13 Most Haunted

IN MASSACHUSETTS

13 Most Haunted

IN MASSACHUSETTS

Sam Baltrusis

CONTENTS

Acknowledgements · vii

Introduction · ix

Chapter 1   S.K. Pierce Mansion, Gardner
Most Haunted: #1 · 1

Chapter 2   Freetown State Forest, Bridgewater Triangle
Most Haunted: #2 · 9

Chapter 3   Hammond Castle, Gloucester
Most Haunted: #3 · 16

Chapter 4   Lizzie Borden's House, Fall River
Most Haunted: #4 · 22

Chapter 5   Houghton Mansion, North Adams
Most Haunted: #5 · 30

Chapter 6   Joshua Ward House, Salem
Most Haunted: #6 · 38

Chapter 7   Longfellow's Wayside Inn, Sudbury
Most Haunted: #7 · 45

Chapter 8   USS Salem, Quincy
Most Haunted: #8 · 52

Chapter 9   Spider Gates Cemetery, Leicester
Most Haunted: #9 · 58

Chapter 10 Boston Light, Little Brewster Island
Most Haunted: #10 · 66

Chapter 11 Witch House, Salem
Most Haunted: #11 · 73

Chapter 12 Victoria House, Provincetown
            Most Haunted: #12 · 79
Chapter 13 Boston Common, Downtown Boston
            Most Haunted: #13 · 84
            Conclusion · 95
            Sources · 109
            About The Author · 113

ACKNOWLEDGEMENTS

After writing *13 Most Haunted in Massachusetts*, I can say without hesitation that this book is my creepiest so far. Even my level-headed copy editor, Andrew Warburton, said he was terrified reading this monster of a project. It's wicked scary. Photographer Frank C. Grace deserves a supernatural slap on the back for capturing the eerie aesthetic of the main haunts in the *13 Most Haunted* countdown. Special thanks to Joni Mayhan, author of *Bones in the Basement*, for penning the introduction. Her wisdom and hands-on experience at several of the state's most-haunted locations is featured throughout the manuscript. I'm grateful Joni and I finally met in person at Houghton Mansion in North Adams. Rob Conti, the new owner of the S.K. Pierce Victorian Mansion in Gardner, also deserves major props for opening his extremely haunted doors to my research team, which included Liz Taegel, co-producer of the video segments in the *13 Most Haunted in Massachusetts* documentary. Thanks to my spirit squad from Boston Haunts and Cambridge Haunts, including Nick Cox, Meaghan Dutton and Hank Fay for helping me rouse the dead and give a voice to those long departed. Major thanks to the handful of paranormal investigators and researchers who helped make *13 Most Haunted in Massachusetts* a reality, including Michael Baker from Para-Boston, my friends and well-respected investigators Rachel Hoffman and Tina Storer from Paranormal Xpeditions and Jeffrey Doucette, a veteran tour guide who appeared in my first book, *Ghosts of Boston: Haunts of the Hub.* My high-school journalism teacher, Beverly Reinschmidt, also deserves kudos for inspiring me to keep writing. Thanks to my mother, Deborah Hughes Dutcher, for being there when I need her most and my friends for their continued support. The team at *MATV's Neighborhood View*, including Anne D'Urso-Rose and Ron Cox, deserve an old-school high five for greenlighting the TV show component of the project. Special thanks to H.P. Lovecraft for his creative use of *Arkham*-inspired phrases like "vaporous corpse-light, yellow and diseased" and Stephen King for terrifying me as a kid with the horror classic, *The Shining*.

INTRODUCTION

"It's the most haunted house in Massachusetts."

—*Joni Mayhan, author and paranormal investigator*

My breath caught in my throat the first time I set eyes on the grand dame. All it took was one glance to know that the mansion was more than a wooden structure. It had a pulse that beat with the current of a thousand souls.

The space next to the front stairwell at the S.K. Pierce Mansion is said to be a portal for the spirits inhabiting the most haunted house in Massachusetts. Author Joni Mayhan said it runs straight up through the building and down into the basement. *Photo by Frank C. Grace.*

The Second Empire Victorian mansion stands on the corner of West Broadway and Union Streets, its faded goldenrod yellow exterior suggesting a troubled past. Built in 1875 by S.K. Pierce, a local furniture mogul, the house has endured many incarnations in its 140-year history. As I researched the house for my book *Bones in the Basement: Surviving the S.K. Pierce Haunted Mansion*, one theme became clear. No matter how hard they tried, no one would ever be truly happy in the house.

When the Pierce family built the mansion, they spared no expenses. It was a masterpiece inside and out. Many famous people visited, including American artist, Norman Rockwell, P.T. Barnum of Barnum and Bailey's Circus fame, and Lieutenant Governor Calvin Coolidge. Esteemed billiards champion Minnesota Fats often joined Pierce for games of billiards in his third floor billiards room. The house was dressed in the Gilded Era finery, with priceless paintings and lavish furniture. Servants bustled back and forth, making their lives easier. It should have been a place where the Pierce family could enjoy their happily-ever-after, but that wasn't in the cards.

Two weeks after moving in, Pierce's wife Susan died of a horrific bacterial infection that destroyed her face and hands before killing her, leaving Pierce a widower with a nearly grown son. After a customary two-year mourning period, Pierce married his second wife Ellen.

Ellen's life should have been complete, but happiness would elude her too. Despite joining all the right social clubs, she was always viewed as Pierce's trophy wife due to their 30-year age difference. If she tried to fit into the community, she continually failed. Even home wasn't a safe haven, due to the rift between her and her stepson Frank, who was only six years her junior.

Ellen provided her husband with two more sons, but found herself mired in more conflict after his death in 1888. Normally, the house and business would have been passed down to the eldest son; however, S.K. Pierce had different plans. He left the house to Ellen and divided the business between her and Frank, something that only served to broaden the gap between the two.

Joni Mayhan said Ellen Pierce's safe on the second-floor
landing is a symbol representing the iron-willed nature of
S.K. Pierce's second wife. *Photo by Frank C. Grace.*

In his attempt to regain control over the house and business, Frank took
his step-mother to court, attempting to gain custody of his two siblings.
Despite losing, he continued to battle with Ellen until her death in 1902.

A testament to Ellen's character, a massive wrought iron safe still
stands in the second-floor landing, emblazoned with her name. Every time
I looked at that safe, I always marveled at the woman who once owned it.
Being a trophy wife in a world filled with arrogance and greed must have
been difficult for her. The mere fact that she had her own safe spoke vol-
umes of her character. Women of her era, especially those deemed as dec-
orations, simply didn't own their own safes. She might have never found
happiness in the mansion, but she always maintained her courage.

After Ellen's death, the sons continued to fight one another in court
for control of the assets. Frank eventually gained possession of the furniture factory, which burned to the ground in 1937, while his younger

brothers delved into the automobile industry, opening up the first Buick and Studebaker dealerships in town. The house was passed down to the youngest son Edward, who opened it up as an inn from 1919 until 1965 when he turned the house over to an eccentric artist named Jay Stemmerman.

By the time Stemmerman purchased the Victorian, it was showing the effects of time and neglect. Stemmerman immediately invested more than $100,000 in the decaying structure, bringing it back to a semblance of its former glory. He used the mansion as a summer home for many years before abandoning it altogether in the mid-1970s. The house sat vacant until 2000 when it was purchased by Mark and Suzanne Veau, who were married inside the mansion.

The Veaus were the first to speak of the haunting. A contractor who was hired to renovate the house began hearing strange sounds while he worked at the house. After he told Mark about his experiences, they brought in two psychic mediums to investigate the happenings. What they found wasn't surprising. The house was haunted by at least six lost souls.

Joni Mayhan spent years researching her book, *Bones in the Basement: Surviving the S.K. Pierce Haunted Victorian Mansion.* The paranormal investigator uncovered secrets and a shadow figure believed to be Edward Pierce in the bowels of the mansion. *Photo by Frank C. Grace.*

The mediums picked up on S.K. Pierce, who was still watching over his mansion, along with an angry man in the basement, a small boy who ran up and down the grand staircase, a prostitute in the Red Room, a man who burned to death in the master bedroom and the former nanny, Mattie Cornwell.

Psychic mediums would describe Mattie Cornwell as the caretaker of the house. They saw her as being in charge, keeping the other lost souls in line. She also prevented other entities from moving into the mansion, turning it into a true ghost hotel. Some speculated that Mattie was in love with S.K. Pierce in life, something that caused her to cling to the mansion after her death at the age of 25.

More perplexing to me was the haunting of the prostitute. Many previous publications stated that the Victorian was once a brothel, something I found to be untrue. Considering prostitution was never legal in the Commonwealth of Massachusetts, the rumor probably stemmed from the period when the mansion was an inn. After Edward's wife Bessie died, the inn quickly fell into obscurity and the clientele became less affluent. Perhaps she met her fate as a visitor of the inn, something that could never be documented. The only women who died inside the Victorian were members of the Pierce family. If she died there, her body was quickly removed and relocated somewhere else.

The ghost of a small boy has been spotted running up and down the grand staircase. *Photo by Frank C. Grace.*

Also confounding to me was the ghost of the little boy. During my years at the Victorian as a guest, I recorded his voice countless times. He always seemed playful and eager to interact with the living. Some suggested that he might have been the son of a servant, who met a tragic end at the mansion. Others believe he was struck and killed by an automobile on the street outside. Considering the fact that no records exist of a little boy dying in the Victorian, his identity will remain a mystery.

I've come to believe that the man in the basement is Edward Pierce. Rumors that he lost the house in a card game ran rampant in the town of Gardner, even though this information could never be substantiated with actual documentation. More than likely, the mansion was in rough shape and Jay Stemmerman, who was a family friend, offered to take the house off of Pierce's hands. Edward was allowed to remain in the mansion as a house guest but chose to live out his last few years in the basement. Despite his gilded beginnings in the mansion, he died a pauper in the mansion his father once built.

The most famous death to have occurred in the Victorian is that of Eino Saari, the son of a Finnish immigrant. Having survived a head injury in World War II, Eino often self-medicated his constant headaches by drinking home-made moonshine. When the Gardner fire department was called to the mansion after reports of flames in the windows, they found Eino burned to death on his bed. Surprisingly, only the bed and occupant were burned. The floors, ceilings and walls were untouched by the fire, leading many to speculate that his death was due to spontaneous combustion. More than likely, the combination of moonshine and cigarette smoking led to the fire, but it wouldn't stop the rumors from circulating.

After purchasing the house in 2000, Mark and Suzanne Veau wouldn't find happiness in the house either. Their union eventually dissolved, forcing them to sell the house when they divorced in 2006.

When Joni Mayhan slept in the Copper Room, she heard footsteps leading up to the bed and then a tap on her shoulder. Some people claim to see a ghostly face on the ceiling of this picture. *Photo by Frank C. Grace.*

When Edwin Gonzalez and Lillian Otero bought the mansion in 2008, they thought they would live there forever, but the hauntings drove them out after only a year and a half. Almost from the beginning, they experienced moving objects, loud bangs and even full body apparitions that appeared out of nowhere. The haunting grew to tremendous proportions, leaving Edwin fearful to be in the house alone. After Lillian was overtaken by an entity in the house, they made the decision to move out, leaving the house empty once more.

In 2015, the mansion was sold again to new owners. Rob and Allison Conti plan to complete the much-needed renovations and then open the house up for rentals. Every October they will dress it up in a Halloween theme for a haunted house attraction.

As I drive past, I still look up at the dark windows, feeling the enduring sadness looming over it. It's truly a house of broken dreams. Despite many good intentions, no one has ever found lasting happiness there. The souls trapped inside continue to linger there, as though they are still searching for the contentment denied to them in life. I hope they eventually find some peace. After everything they've endured, they certainly deserve it.

Joni Mayhan is a paranormal investigator and the author of 13 books, including *Bones in the Basement: Surviving the S.K. Pierce Haunted Victorian Mansion.* To learn more about Mayhan, please visit her website: Jonimayhan.com.

Chapter 1

S.K. PIERCE MANSION
GARDNER
MOST HAUNTED: #1

"I was told by intuitives that the spirits in the house have something very important to tell me. Does that sound crazy?"

—Rob Conti, *S.K. Pierce Victorian Mansion's new owner*

A woman named Mattie Cornwell summoned me to this house. She's been dead for more than a century.

In the recurring dream, I see her silhouette from a gold-colored Victorian's second floor. She's upset. I can see an outline of what looks like a tightly wound bun in her hair. Her clothing is late 1800s school marm and she looks much older than her actual age. I would guess she's in her 20s. The woman is a caretaker of sorts and is protecting the home from forces out of her control. She's losing the battle and is calling me from the light for help.

Think Mary Poppins but without the spoonful of sugar. In my dream, she's serving up daggers.

Something horrible happened in that house and she is begging the living to help her. I could hear her singing a folk song from the window. She was throwing books and papers at me from the home's second floor. She's saying what I remember as "sefnock" over and over at a shadowy man who is in the room with her. I'm terrified.

My dream of Mattie was in 2011. I was writing what would become my first book, *Ghosts of Boston: Haunts of the Hub.* I initially thought she was the "stay behind" spirit, the seamstress I lovingly called "scissor sister," who haunted my home in Somerville's Davis Square.

I was wrong.

The dream was prophetic in a way. I didn't make a connection to the haunted S.K. Pierce Victorian Mansion in Gardner until I saw a photo of the structure posted online in late 2014. My friends Rachel Hoffman and Tina Storer from Paranormal Xpeditions were investigating the location and I had a severe reaction when I saw a post from the Victorian structure because I'd seen it repeatedly in my dreams.

I swore I would never go there. But here I am—going to the very spot where Mattie Cornwell once lived. What was I thinking?

A friend who has intuitive abilities warned me about the shadow figure in my dreams. "That woman will suck the air out of you," she said during an online chat. "No. I mean it. Like sitting on your chest. You won't be able to inhale." She said the spirit's name is Maddie or Matilda.

I found out recently from fellow author Joni Mayhan that the former nanny at the haunted S.K. Pierce Victorian was named Mattie Cornwell. Her spirit has been in the house since the late 1800s. "Petite, with long dark hair that she wore in a bun, she once cared for the Pierce children," wrote Mayhan in *Bones In The Basement.* "Chores were scheduled at specific times, and the children were taught to behave. Even though she was long dead, she remained the protector of the house, keeping it safe from trespassers and ensuring the other resident ghosts behaved themselves."

Mayhan said Cornwell had crossed over and is no longer bound to the haunted Victorian. "She was the Pierce family's nanny. Mattie wasn't negative though. She was the gatekeeper and peacekeeper there, but she was inadvertently crossed over during a house cleansing in 2011," Mayhan told me. "After she left, the really nasty ones came in. There are a few nasty female entities there, but Mattie isn't one of them."

#1

The S.K. Pierce Mansion is located at 4 West Broadway in Gardner. *Photo by Frank C. Grace.*

According to Mayhan's *Bones In The Basement*, Cornwell died young. "She was born in 1859 in Nova Scotia, Canada. She was 21 when she came to work for the Pierce family as a servant in the house. Her primary focus was caring for the Pierce children. She was firm but loving with the children, keeping them mindful of their manners and helping them grow into the influential men they would one day become," wrote Mayhan. "Later research would show that Mattie died at the young age of twenty-five from an acute inflammation of the hip just two years after getting married. Her tragedy would be just one among many at the Victorian mansion. It was as if the house collected them, like some people collected old coins."

Rachel Hoffman, my friend from the all-female investigation team Paranormal Xpeditions, said I should be wary about the haunted house in Gardner. "You might not be able to walk in," explained Hoffman. "I swear it's a pressure cooker. You will feel it as soon as you see it. Look into the top window and tell me what you see. Then I'll tell you."

The ghost of the Haunted Victorian's caretaker and nanny Mattie Cornwell summoned sensitives to the S.K. Pierce Mansion, begging the living to help her. *Photo by Frank C. Grace.*

Hoffman, who was featured in a taped investigation at the mansion with Tina Storer and her sister, Danielle Medina, said the experience still haunts her. She believes the location is a portal, a vortex of sorts to the spirit world that allows both good and bad spirits to cross over. "There's more than one story there," she said. "There's a story for every step you take."

When PXP was investigating the mansion in late 2014, I had a strong psychic feeling that one of the investigators, Tina Storer, wasn't safe. I sent a message to the PXP team warning them. Hoffman told me later that Storer had to be escorted out of the building because she couldn't breathe. It was like the spirits were taking the air out of her lungs.

"Tina had issues where the man was burned," Hoffman told me. "At one point, she did feel protected. But it was so intense. Our temp gage was 66.6."

Medina, Hoffman's sister, was pregnant during the investigation and the group uncovered an electromagnetic voice phenomenon, or EVP, in the nursery. "We got my pregnant sister bending over to pick up a baby in the nursery and the ovilus said 'mama,'" explained Hoffman. "My sister is a skeptic so this was profound."

Hoffman and the PXP team smudged the location with a cleansing ritual involving coffin nails and sweet grass. The usual ceremony with the old standby sage simply didn't work. "When closing out a paranormal investigation, we sometimes use coffin nails," Hoffman explained. "I found our container used in the haunted Victorian Mansion with the bottom half of the glass jar totally gone. I wouldn't be surprised to find the nails we pounded in the ground embedded in a tree. Renovations and hands switching is stirring up the activity majorly."

Yes, construction notoriously conjures up the long departed. Apparently, spirits don't like change.

Rob Conti, the ringleader behind the New Jersey-based Dark Carnival and a dentist during the day, said he always wanted to own a standalone haunted attraction. The S.K. Pierce mansion was literally ripped from his childhood fantasies. He says the fact that the 7,000-square-foot mansion located at 4 Broadway in Gardner is "certified haunted" is an added bonus.

"Since I was 15, I always wanted a single-family haunted house," he said. "I always had a picture in my mind of what that attraction would look like. As I got older, I tried to make this vision a reality but there were regulations in New Jersey that prohibited it."

Conti, who actually didn't visit the Victorian until the day he closed the sale on the building, said a friend posted the real estate listing for the mansion on his Facebook page. "As soon as I saw it, I knew the image of the house was the image I had in my head for the past 25 years."

The new owner said he will hash out the details after the year-long renovations, but he plans to rent out the unit for 11 months of the year and will turn the space into a haunted attraction every October. Since purchasing what paranormal experts believe is the most haunted house in Massachusetts, Conti said he has been contacted by all sorts of people.

"I've been told that the spirits in the house knew who I was before I even called," he said, sort of creeped out by the idea. "Apparently, I'm liked by the spirits in the house, which is a good thing, I hope."

Conti also had a paranormal experience after walking into the structure's dining room, the same spot investigators believe is a portal. "I started feeling dizzy and had to be escorted out of the building," he explained. Also, the Dark Carnival owner said a contractor, who didn't know the building's haunted history, told him that somebody else was on the second floor when there was no one else in the house.

"I was also told by intuitives that the spirits in the house have something very important to tell me," Conti continued. "Does that sound crazy?"

Actually, no.

As I stand gazing at the house that haunted my dreams for years, I replay the dream of the woman I believe to be Mattie Cornwell looking out of the second-floor window. As I walk closer to my nightmare, I'm shivering in the beauty and the madness of the moment. I think about the word "sefnock" that she chanted over and over. I hit my head as I quickly jump into the car near the S.K. Pierce Mansion's driveway searching for a notepad. I write the mystery word out phonetically.

Author Sam Baltrusis stands in front of the "most haunted house in Massachusetts," the S.K. Pierce Mansion in Gardner. *Photo by Frank C. Grace.*

Then I had an epiphany. I gasped for air. The woman's cryptic, post-mortem plea is backwards. She's demanding that the shadow figure … confess.

Cars are driving by and passengers are yelling things at me like "there's someone behind you" and "this place is really, really haunted." My cellphone starts to flip out and, mysteriously, seems to have a mind of its own, calling random people from my contact list. I hear what sounds like a disembodied male voice whispering in my ear: "Get out of here."

I look again at the second-floor window, expecting to see Mattie Cornwell, the spirit who mistakenly crossed to the light years ago. Instead, I see a black bird, possibly a crow or a dark-colored pigeon, perched on the ledge. The white-lace curtains move as if someone is peering out of the window.

I can't breathe.

Chapter 2

FREETOWN STATE FOREST
BRIDGEWATER TRIANGLE
MOST HAUNTED: #2

"If you were a victim, I don't know how you would escape the clutches of a murderer out there. It seems like the forest could swallow you ... and it has to."

—RACHEL HOFFMAN, PXP'S "TRUE CRIME PARANORMAL"

The so-called Bridgewater Triangle, an area of about 200 square miles in Southeastern Massachusetts, is an epicenter of the Commonwealth's alleged paranormal activity and over-the-top urban legends. Tales associated with the Triangle include: Native American curses; satanic cults; a redheaded hitchhiker; a swamp called Hockomock, which the Wampanoag tribe believed was "the place where spirits dwell"; numerous UFO sightings, including one as far back as 1760; three-foot cryptids known as Pukwudgies; and the Assonet Ledge in Freetown State Forest, where visitors report seeing ghosts standing, jumping and inexplicably disappearing.

Of all of the hocus pocus occurring on the spooky South Coast, the most spine-tingling story about the Bridgewater Triangle is the real-life horror that unfolded in Freetown State Forest in November 1978. The decomposed body of Mary Lou Arruda, a teen cheerleader from nearby Raynham, was discovered tied to a tree in the forest. The murdered girl was 15 years old. She disappeared in the afternoon of Sept. 8, 1978. A newspaper delivery boy found her bicycle near the scene. She was missing for two months.

James M. Kater, a 32-year-old donut maker from Brockton, was indicted in connection with the Arruda murder. His green car was spotted in Raynham and his vehicle had a nine-inch gash in the front that matched the girl's bicycle. He was also on probation for a similar incident in 1968 when he kidnapped a girl from Andover. Kater has stood trial four times and his final appeal was rejected by the U.S. Supreme Court in 2007. He is currently serving his sentence in federal prison in California.

According to trial documents, "Arruda had been alive and in a standing position when she was tied to the tree." Once she became unconscious, the weight of her head against the ligature around her neck caused her to suffocate. While there are no ties to her murder and the alleged reports of satanic cult activity in Freetown State Forest, the case reinforced the idea that the area is cursed.

"The Town of Freetown was purchased in 1659 from the Wampanoag Tribe and the town was incorporated in 1683. The Native Americans believed the land was highly sacred when Wamsutta sold it, possibly without the backing of the tribe, maybe the cause of the evil energy," reported the SouthCoast Ghost paranormal group online. "Many believe that events of the area have turned the once gentle spirits violent, attracting evil to it and the forest in return is being fed by the evil. Native Americans claim the horrible crimes and hauntings will not stop until the tribe is given back the land."

People who stumble on the location where Arruda's body was found say it's paranormally active. "I have seen shadow people," reported an anonymous paranormal investigator on the *Unexplained Mysteries* forum. "I have seen a spirit of a girl near the site where they found Mary Lou Arruda's body in 1978. I recently spent the entire night in the forest with my group. We had some people feel like they were pushed. We heard laughter in the woods. Occasionally we heard groans, breathing and screams." The source reported seeing lights like softball-sized fireflies at the top of the trees. "One from our group swore she saw someone jumping from tree to tree but it was unverified."

Located five minutes from Fall River and Taunton, the extremely haunted Freetown State Forest is located in the lower-right corner of the Bridgewater Triangle. *Photo by Frank C. Grace.*

Another source on *Unexplained Mysteries* echoed claims about the negative energy associated with the forest. "I had the distinct feeling we were being followed and watched," he confirmed. "I could have sworn I saw people in the woods."

One year after the Arruda murder, all hell broke loose in the cursed Freetown State Forest. Karen Marsden, a woman believed to be a prostitute in Fall River, was savagely murdered. Carl Drew, a self-proclaimed devil worshipper and pimp, supposedly led ritualistic gatherings in the forest at a place known as the Ice Shack. The so-called "son of Satan" was also accused of three cult-like murders.

"Drew was on trial for the February 1980 murder of Karen Marsden, a Fall River prostitute whose skull and other remains were found in a wooded area of Westport in April the same year," reported *SouthCoast Today*. "While on trial for Marsden's murder, he was also under indictment for the October 1979 killing of Doreen Levesque, another Fall River prostitute."

Robin Murphy, an 18-year-old sex worker who was granted immunity to testify against Drew, claimed the man organized at least 10 satanic gatherings, which led to three ritualistic murders. "At the trial, Murphy said that she, Drew and two others had driven Marsden to a wooded area of Westport where they got out of the car and Murphy began dragging Marsden through the woods by her throat and hair," explained *SouthCoast Today*. "Drew told Marsden to give Murphy a ring she was wearing but she refused so Drew cut her finger off to get it."

Murphy, who claimed to have been possessed by Satan, said she slit Marsden's throat because the cult leader demanded it. Murphy testified that Drew carved an "X" in the murdered woman's chest and started speaking in a demonic tongue. He then dabbed the mutilated woman's blood on his fingers and marked an "X" on Murphy's forehead, telling her that the sacrifice was an initiation into his cult. Murphy said two other murders, including the savage slaughter of Levesque, were eerily similar.

Séances using the skulls of the victims were supposedly held, according to Murphy, in the Freetown State Forest. "The killing of Doreen

Levesque was an offering of the soul to Satan and so was the killing of Miss Marsden," Murphy said to the court. Drew is still in prison for the three murders he was accused of inciting 25 years ago.

Inspired by the Drew case, Freetown State Forest became a hotbed of black mass gatherings in the '80s. One man, William LaFrance was found camping in the forest with rows of yellow candles and satanic symbols carved in the dirt. Officers found "666" tacked to the tree near LaFrance's car. Park rangers claimed that the haunted Assonet Ledge was also plagued with freshly painted satanic symbols, skulls and pentagrams in the late '80s. For the record, visitors still claim to encounter spirits at the abandoned quarry, which is believed to be the site of multiple suicides over the years.

The ranger station, a cabin-like structure built in the 1940s for loggers in the forest, is where a lot of the cult activity is believed to have taken place. People who claimed to have seen the wooden structure said it's where Carl Drew held his infamous drug-induced séances. Animal bones have been found in the area near the hijacked shack. There's also a structure known as the "Ice Shack" but it's commonly mistaken for the ranger station.

There was also a bunker in the Freetown State Forest. Rangers found pentagrams and evidence of ritualistic gatherings in the culvert-style cave. Officers believed the bunker was evil. However, former members of the Society of Creative Anachronism (SCA) claimed it was a gathering spot for neo-pagan and Wiccan practitioners and not followers of the devil.

In addition to all the alleged cult activity, a ghostly trucker has been spotted regularly on Copicut Road in the heart of Freetown State Forest. He supposedly blares his horn and threatens passing motorists who venture into the forest at night.

There's a site called Profile Rock that looks like a man's face carved in a granite outcropping. Lore suggested that it was the face of the great Native American sachem, Chief Massasoit, leader of the Wampanoag people. He's responsible for saving the Pilgrims in Plymouth from starvation by offering corn to the dying settlers.

Whether Freetown State Forest is actually haunted or not, there's no denying it's freakishly macabre history. As someone who has spent time in the forest, there's definitely an eerie electricity that permeates the 5,217-acre area. There was a massive fire in the woods in March 1976 that damaged 500 acres and another in September 1980 that destroyed 230 acres.

In addition to the murders in the late '70s, more deaths occurred, including that of a drifter who was killed in 1987 after being mistaken as an undercover police officer. Two men were shot to death on Bell Rock Road in 2001 and there were two assaults in 1991 and 1998.

Rachel Hoffman and Tina Storer produced a documentary on Freetown in 2014 for their *True Crime Paranormal* series. The ghost-hunting team said the serene forest turned nightmarish after dark. The Bay State's most haunted forest? Both investigators believe the Freetown State Forest is a hotbed of primordial evil. It's almost as if the forest somehow devours its victims.

"The negative energy this place is well known for makes you so susceptible to energy being sucked out of you," explained Storer.

Hoffman agreed. "It wasn't hard for us to see how bodies could be hidden for three to six months at a time," Hoffman continued. "The forest is extremely dense and the drop offs are extremely high. The highway goes in all different directions. If you were a victim, I don't know how you would escape the clutches of a murderer out there. It seems like the forest could swallow you … and it has to."

But is it haunted? Absolutely. It's as if the Freetown State Forest has a devilish mind of its own.

Assonet Ledge in Freetown State Forest is where visitors report seeing ghosts standing, jumping and inexplicably disappearing. *Photo by Frank C. Grace.*

Chapter 3

HAMMOND CASTLE
GLOUCESTER
MOST HAUNTED: #3

*"The big story about this place when I was a kid is
that Hammond himself haunted the grounds."*

—JOSH GATES, "GHOST HUNTERS" GUEST INVESTIGATOR

When my friend and research assistant Andrew Warburton and I visited Hammond Castle in Gloucester back in July 2012, I heard a disembodied voice say "look" in the library, which historians call the "whisper" room. It led me to a picture of Henry Davis Sleeper.

Was it Sleeper's ghost? Probably not. However, I wouldn't be surprised if it was the structure's former owner trying to reach out to me to let me know that his friend Sleeper had designed the room.

Inventor John Hays Hammond, Jr. built this breathtaking medieval-style castle in the late 1920s. Marrying his wife Irene Fenton late in his life, the eccentric gentleman used the mansion as a laboratory and private residence until his death in 1956. In fact, he's buried in a crypt tucked away on the property and is rumored to be among the several wayward spirits who haunt the house. Hammond had an odd desire to be reincarnated as a cat and many believe the black feline who roamed the grounds and set up shop in his favorite chair in the library was, in fact, Hammond himself.

Hammond Castle is located at 80 Hesperus Ave.
in Gloucester. *Photo by Ryan Miner.*

The mad scientist collected bizarre antiques, like the skull of a seaman from Christopher Columbus' crew, and it's said that some of the artifacts are enchanted. He was also fascinated by spiritualism and there's an area known as the "dead spot," marked by a chair, where Hammond hosted psychic mediums. Items in the castle inexplicably disappear and reappear. A full-bodied apparition has been seen in the organ loft and a red-haired female specter has popped up among guests at weddings held at the castle.

Henry Davis Sleeper, the legendary designer who built Eastern Point's Beauport, was a regular at Hammond Castle. In fact, Sleeper designed the inventor's favorite spot, known as the "whisper room," where people have heard disembodied voices from beyond.

I first visited the haunted castle a few weeks before Syfy's *Ghost Hunters* was slotted to investigate. Oddly, two days after my initial trip to Gloucester, I was scheduled to interview one of the show's hosts, Adam Berry, in Provincetown. He was preparing for a top-secret shoot.

"Are you investigating Hammond Castle?" I asked Berry. He nodded but couldn't give any details. He was shocked that I intuitively knew that *Ghost Hunters* was heading to Gloucester.

For the record, I did get a heads up from John Pettibone, the curator and director of the haunted hot spot. But I was also mysteriously called to the location. Pettibone was a bit freaked out when I told him that I write historical-based ghost books and asked if the castle was paranormally active. "Is the castle haunted? We'll find out in a few weeks," Pettibone told me in 2012. "The team from TAPS is doing the investigation. I feel strongly that Hammond would have approved of their scientific approach to paranormal investigations."

Pettibone told me that Hammond and his wife were ghost hunters before the fad became a pop culture phenomenon. In many ways, the couple were trailblazers paving the way for respected, contemporary investigators like The Atlantic Paranormal Society.

"Hammond firmly believed that when you bring back architectural items that you're bringing back the spirit of the original owner," Pettibone explained to the TAPS team on Syfy's *Ghost Hunters*. "John Hammond did paranormal experiments using his Faraday Cage. His wife was an astrologer and a psychic. They did séances here. We had John Hammond seen by a school group on the balcony in the Great Hall. We had his wife seen at a window."

The episode, which aired in November 2012, was a throwback to the old-school *Ghost Hunters* investigations that presented some convincing evidence. Josh Gates, host of Syfy's *Destination Truth* and the Travel Channel's *Expedition Unknown*, joined the team and confirmed that he grew up close to Gloucester in nearby Manchester-by-the-Sea. "There's always been ghost stories here since I was a kid. I almost had my prom here," Gates joked. "It was deemed too scary to have a prom at so we didn't."

According to Pettibone, guests in the library or "whisper room" report hearing voices speaking foreign languages. Books from Hammond's collection of the occult have flown off shelves without explanation. Visitors have also taken mysterious photos in the Great Hall of what looked liked orbs with distinct heads.

Employees told the *Ghost Hunters* team that Hammond's medieval bedroom on the second floor is also extremely active. "Some people who walk in there feel really uneasy," said Hammond Castle employee Linda Rose. "They feel cool. Their hair would stand up on end. There was another gentleman that went in there and felt something go through him."

Jay Craveiro, also a staffer at the Hammond Castle, said a girl with a tour group had a face-to-face encounter with a spirit on the second floor near the medieval bedroom. According to Craveiro, her blood-curdling scream echoed throughout the castle. "She said she saw a hand reach toward her face while the staff was downstairs," Craveiro explained. "She just started running all the way through the castle and right out of the front door. She refused to come back into the building."

In addition to the eyewitness accounts, there's a series of photos of what appears to be a full-bodied apparition walking up the castle's staircase. "It has a little bit of a definition and when you put the photos together it appears to move up the steps almost as if you can see an end of a pant leg moving its foot up each step," remarked Kris Gurksnis, a Salem-based visitor to Hammond Castle.

The TAPS team's actual investigation of the historic structure is arguably one of the *Ghost Hunters* crew's more entertaining shows in recent years. In its show recap, Syfy reported the following: "During the investigation, Dave and Tango hear a voice, while Amy and Adam hear a voice and whistling in the room with them. Meanwhile, K.J. and Britt have great communication with a spirit using a rim pod. Not only do Jason and Steve hear strange voices behind them, but also feet walking behind them."

To reiterate the myth that Hammond would reincarnate as a feline, a cat appeared out of nowhere during the investigation. "Josh and Ashley get some great responses to their questions on the K2 meter, and actually give chase to a voice. When they move to the library, the chandelier begins swinging aggressively without any cause," Syfy described. "As Josh says, it's like a cliché haunted house."

Inventor John Hays Hammond, Jr. was buried on the grounds of his medieval-style castle. The eccentric had an odd desire to be reincarnated as a cat and many believe he succeeded. *Photo by Ryan Miner.*

When asked how the investigation was unfolding, Gates said "it was awesome. We heard voices and one of them came two feet behind us. I was able to register what it was and where it was coming from and still hear and analyze it," the TV host said. "All of the different teams are having similar experiences. It's a good, all-round case for everybody."

Gates was right. The K2 meter lit up on command during a call-and-response session near the so-called "dead spot" in the Great Hall. There was also a recording of residual chatter of what clearly sounded like a cocktail party from another era. The moving chandelier was a bit shocking during Ashley Troub and Gates's trek through the Great Hall.

"The big story about this place when I was a kid is that Hammond himself haunted the grounds," Gates said during the investigation.

When Jason Hawes and Steve Gonsalves turned on their digital recorder, they picked up a Class A electronic-voice phenomenon. It was a male voice and it clearly said: "Hammond." Pettibone was visibly excited when he heard the EVP during the reveal. "I don't hear it as a question," the curator responded. "I hear it as a statement."

Pettibone said he was convinced by the TAPS crew's findings. "Is John Hammond still here? Is Irene still here? I am just amazed what came out," Pettibone gushed. "Someone is trying to let us know they're still here."

Chapter 4

LIZZIE BORDEN'S HOUSE
FALL RIVER
MOST HAUNTED: #4

"Keep on killing. Keep 'em coming."

—*"Ghost Adventures" EVP from Lizzie Borden's House*

Although she was tried and acquitted of the gruesome murder at her 1845-era Victorian home located at 92 2nd St. in Fall River, the axe-wielding Lizzie Borden never shook her "forty whacks" claim to fame that she hacked up her father and stepmother on August 4, 1892. In addition to her chop-chop notoriety, Borden apparently had an intimate relationship with actress Nance O'Neill.

There's also a theory that she had a torrid love affair with the house-keeper, Bridget Sullivan, and their testimony contradicted each other during the trial and sometimes even contradicted their own stories.

Currently a bed and breakfast and museum, the Borden house is open for curiosity seekers to spend the night in the actual house where the murders took place.

#4

The Lizzie Borden house, now a bed and breakfast, is located at 92 Second St. in Fall River. *Photo by Frank C. Grace.*

As far as ghosts are concerned, visitors claim to hear sounds of a woman weeping and have spotted a full-bodied apparition wearing Victorian-era clothing dusting the furniture. There are also reports of phantom footsteps storming down the stairs and doors mysteriously opening and closing. Also, guests have heard muffled conversations coming from vacant rooms. Perhaps it's the spirits of Borden and Sullivan making a post-mortem pact to hide the bloody hatchet.

Or, maybe it's something more sinister?

I have had spirit communication dreams about two locations featured in *13 Most Haunted in Massachusetts*. One was about the S.K. Pierce Haunted Victorian in Gardner. The other was Lizzie Borden's House in Fall River.

In the dream, I saw a man with 1800s-era clothing and facial hair walk into a house with flowery wallpaper. He takes off his hat and sits on an old-school couch. The dream looked like a black-and-white 35mm and unfolded slower than the typical silent-era film. Before the man could rest his head, he looked at me and subtitles appeared, as if I was watching a film from the early 1900s. A woman appeared holding a hatchet behind her back.

The subtitle that appeared in the dream haunted me for years. It read: "Diablo did it." Then I woke up.

I didn't figure out the correlation between the house and my dream until I visited the Lizzie Borden House in 2011 while on assignment for a magazine. At the time, I was more interested in trying to solve the murder and was less focused on the message in my dream.

In hindsight, my dream seemed to be implying that the murderer—whether it was Lizzie, Bridget Sullivan or even the uncle John V. Morse—was possessed by a demonic entity.

The crew from *Ghost Adventures* investigated the house in 2011. I recently watched the episode online. The interesting part of the investigation was the paranormal research by Jeff Belanger.

"Andrew and Abby weren't even the first two Bordens to die on that property," Belanger explained. "In 1848, Andrew's uncle lived in the house right next door. His wife went nuts and drowned her three children in a well. One lived. Then she took her own life with a straight razor, slit her throat."

Lizzie Borden never shook her "forty whacks" claim to fame. For the record, Borden's step-mother was struck 18 or 19 times with an axe and her father suffered 11 blows on the couch. *Photo by Frank C. Grace.*

The investigation explored the possibility of an evil entity and the idea that the "property is plagued with dark spirits." I believe this is likely. The electronic voice phenomenon the trio allegedly captured upstairs is terrifying to me. It said: "Keep on killing. Keep 'em coming."

Another message from the spirit box said: "Tell 'em about the girl."

What girl? It's believed that Andrew Borden was communicating a message during the séance and that the message had something to do with the theory, which the psychic medium in *Ghost Adventures* discussed, that the father had an incestuous relationship with Lizzie after her mother, Sarah, died. The girl may have been one of Borden's lesbian lovers.

The uncle, John V. Morse, testified in court that the night before the murder, Lizzie had an unidentified guest in her room. He never spotted the mystery guest nor commented on the person's gender.

The murder in 1848 has fueled discussions of madness possibly running in the Borden family. In fact, the infanticide by Eliza Darling Borden was actually brought up in Lizzie's highly publicized trial. It's believed that Eliza drowned her children in the cellar's cistern and then, possibly suffering from postpartum depression, took her own life by cutting her throat with a straight razor.

For the record, Lizzie wasn't a blood relative of Eliza and was connected to her only by marriage through her great-uncle Lawdwick.

The children, who died 44 years before Abby and Andrew were murdered, are rumored to haunt the Lizzie Borden House. Guests leave dolls and other toys for ghost children who are believed to inhabit the guest rooms. There are also reports of children laughing on the second and third floors.

Another explanation of the "tell 'em about the girl" spirit-box message on *Ghost Adventures* is that it could be a reference to the murdered child, Eliza Ann Borden, who was two when she was drowned in the basement of 96 2nd St.

In other words, the girl the spirit-box message was referring to may be a ghost child.

Lee-ann Wilber, proprietor of the Lizzie Borden House, told the Bio Channel that it's common for guests to run out of the inn in fright. "I'm not used to picking up on things. They just sort of blend in now," Wilber said. "Nothing to drive me out of here."

However, in 2004 she was scared out of the house. She fell asleep on the parlor room's couch and woke at 3 a.m. and saw a shadow person. The old-school chandelier was responsible for the black mist in the hallway, she believed, but noticed a misty figure move up the staircase.

"And as I'm looking at it, it walked up the staircase," Wilber told the Bio Channel. "I said to no one in particular, 'You win tonight,' and went to sleep in my car."

Investigators at the crime scene didn't find any bloody clothing. However, Lizzie Borden burned a dress in the stove, saying she brushed up against fresh paint and it ruined her dress. *Photo by Frank C. Grace.*

Wilber said she was a skeptic when she moved in more than a decade ago. "Living here," said Wilber, "very quickly, I became a believer."

Because of its gory history, it's no surprise that the Lizzie Borden House is believed to be haunted. There have been numerous reports of cold spots in the master bedroom where Abby came face-to-face with her cold-blooded killer. There's also lore involving a former maid who quit after seeing a body-shaped indentation on the bed in Abby's room.

However, the ghostly reports have turned dark in the past few years.

My fear is that the *Ghost Adventures* lockdown may have stirred up negative energy within the house ... or possibly brought in evil from outside the building. According to several sources, the place became unusually active after the investigation.

Rachel Hoffman from *Paranormal Xpeditions* agreed that the crew of *Ghost Adventures* potentially conjured up activity. The paranormal investigator visited the property the day after the *GAC* lockdown. "I went to Lizzie's house and opened the door and 100 black flies flew out—grown flies," Hoffman explained. "They left six hours before."

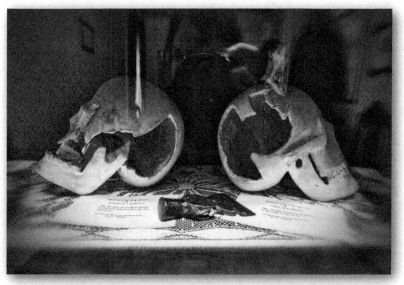

Currently a bed and breakfast and museum, Borden's house is open for curiosity seekers to spend the night in the actual location where the murders took place. *Photo by Frank C. Grace.*

Flies, as well as shadow people, are common in a house demonstrating demonic activity. Nausea, reported by Zak Bagans and Nick Groff on *Ghost Adventures*, is also a sign of a dark force. Abby, Andrew and the maid, Bridget, and even Lizzie reported nausea hours before the two murders in 1892. Temperature fluctuations, specifically in a localized area like Abby's bedroom, have been reported in other cases of demonic infestation.

Hoffman, who has investigated the Lizzie Borden House several times, said she's had experiences in the basement with her colleague Tina Storer. She also believes that Lizzie's stepmother Abby is active in the house. "I think that Abigail is there and she was indicating to us that it was an employee of her husband that murdered them," Hoffman explained. "Harper was a name we got in the basement."

In the inquest testimony of Lizzie, she mentions a nameless man who visited the house within two weeks of the double homicide. "I did not see anything. I heard the bell ring and father went to the door and let him in," Borden testified. "I did not hear anything for some time except just the voices. Then I heard the man say, 'I would like to have that place; I would like to have that store.' Father said, 'I am not willing to let your business go in there.' They talked a while and then their voices were louder and I heard father order him out and went to the front door with him."

Borden couldn't identify the out-of-town visitor. However, he should have been a person of interest.

Did Lizzie Borden do it? We'll probably never know for sure. However, it may have been dark forces conjured in the house that inspired her to do the ghastly deed. The devil once roamed here. He's waiting in the shadows of the Lizzie Borden House, patiently plotting a return.

Chapter 5

HOUGHTON MANSION
NORTH ADAMS
MOST HAUNTED: #5

"I knew there was a dark entity in the basement of the mansion. We encountered him there several times before and saw him in the form of dark shadows moving in the darkness."

—JONI MAYHAN, AUTHOR AND PARANORMAL INVESTIGATOR

Sensitives claim to have an inexplicable feeling of sadness when they enter the Houghton Mansion in North Adams. Based on my brief but memorable visit to the haunted location, it's a bit overwhelming walking into the majestic old house built by Albert C. Houghton, a millionaire and North Adam's first mayor. It's almost as if the guilt associated with a tragedy in 1914 has psychically imprinted itself onto the walls of the historic Masonic Temple located at 172 Church St.

So, what happened more than a century ago to the Houghton family?

It all started with a casual drive at 9 a.m. on August 1, 1914. What happened next caused a ripple effect that destroyed the family and left an indelible mark on the mansion. Houghton asked his employee, John Widders, to rev up their new Pierce-Arrow touring car and drive his family and friends along the winding roads that cut through the picturesque mountains of North Adams. Houghton's wife, Cordelia, decided to stay home that fateful day.

The Albert C. Houghton mansion is now a Masonic Temple located at 172 Church St. in North Adams. *Photo by Frank C. Grace.*

While they were en route to Bennington, Vermont, Widders hit a soft shoulder on the road after swerving around a team of horses. The car then tumbled down an embankment and flipped three times. The men, including Houghton and Widders, escaped with minor injuries.

The patriarch's daughter, Mary, died in the North Adams hospital immediately after the impact and so did her childhood friend, Sybil Hutton. Widders, overwhelmed with grief, lifted a horse pistol to his temple and committed suicide in the cellar of the mansion's barn. Houghton, who was expected to survive the accident, returned to his home and died ten days later. His injuries from the car crash were fatal but many believe he actually died from heartbreak after losing his beloved daughter so tragically.

Paranormal investigators claim that an aura of destruction has psychically imprinted itself on the Houghton Mansion.

I visited the location in early August, a few days after the 101-year anniversary of the Houghton tragedy, and was immediately overwhelmed with sadness. Joni Mayhan, author of *Bones in the Basement* and featured investigator of the evening, said it's common for sensitives to pick up on the energy still lingering in the home. My *13 Most Haunted* documentary crew interviewed the author minutes before her overnight investigation.

"It's very active," Mayhan told me. "The last time I was here I actually saw an apparition in the basement. It was the bottom of a little girl's dress. In the past, we've caught a lot of EVPs here."

After we left, she said all hell broke loose during what was her fifth visit to the North Adams hot spot.

"I was well-versed on the history and had a good idea what to expect," Mayhan explained on her blog. "While I was excited to be returning to one of my favorite haunts, I was looking forward to the social aspect more than the actual haunting. I would be in for a shock. My fifth visit was a wild ride I will never forget."

Mayhan told me that before the investigation, she wasn't convinced the mansion was one of the Bay State's most haunted locations. However, her tune quickly changed. After the investigation, she was convinced that something much darker had made a home for itself in the bowels of the Houghton Mansion.

Paranormal investigators, including the crew from the Travel Channel's *Ghost Adventures*, claim that an aura of destruction has psychically imprinted itself on the Houghton Mansion. *Photo by Frank C. Grace.*

"I knew there was a dark entity in the basement of the mansion. We encountered him there several times before and saw him in the form of dark shadows moving in the darkness," Mayhan explained. "There was also supposed to be a little girl there who answers to the name Laura. While the Houghtons had a daughter named Laura who died at the age of three, many aren't convinced this is the same little girl. They theorize that the mansion was built on an existing foundation, so the ghost of the child could belong to the first house that sat on the property."

Mayhan said she saw a dark shadow pacing back and forth in front of a doorway in the basement.

"As we settled into the session, the mediums in the group could feel an energy building. The darkness grew to epic proportions, filling the room with a sense of anger and loathing that even the non-mediums could feel," Mayhan recalled. "At one point, one member of the group became so overwhelmed with the dark energy, she needed to remove herself from the building to recoup her energy."

Mayhan picked up an EVP that could be labeled as Class A. The disembodied voice said: "sit down." Based on the tone of the recording, the energy sounded aggressive.

The insults continued in Mary Houghton's bedroom. The EVPs Mayhan captured were overtly antagonistic. A male voice insulted one of the women in the room and called another investigator a "fat bastard." After a psychic identified an older female spirit hiding in the corner and asked who was standing before her, the male voice spoke through the spirit box saying that "it's that poor bitch."

On the third floor, there's a locker room that was used by the Masons after they purchased the mansion in the 1920s. The women felt uncomfortable on the third-floor and when Mayhan asked if they should leave the locker room, an EVP responded: "if you could."

The crew from the Travel Channel's *Ghost Adventures* had an equally memorable "lockdown" when they investigated the Houghton Mansion in 2008.

"Nestled in the heart of the Berkshire Mountains is one of New England's most mysterious and haunted buildings," said Zak Bagans. "Before we get locked down, I want to learn about the history. There's a lot of dark history about this place and I hear there are some tragic events that happened to the family that built this place, the Houghton family. They're the ones said to haunt this place," adding that the mansion is home to a Masonic Temple but its "dark history began in the early 1900s."

The masons who frequent the location confirmed the hauntings to Bagans. "Nearly every time I come down you hear a door slam or footsteps," said Nick Montello. Mason Randy Ransford said doors mysteriously open and close when no one else is there.

One of the masons told Bagans that the property is lined with granite boulders taken from the Hoosac Tunnel, also known as the "bloody pit."

Bagans intimated that the Houghton tragedy could have been somehow tied to those rocks.

Mayhan told me that Bagan's "Hoosac Tunnel curse" theory is definitely viable. "Yes, it's possible that all of the negative energy, all of the death and destruction in the Hoosac Tunnel was somehow absorbed and then transferred here."

Michael Norman and Beth Scott wrote about the curses associated with the so-called "bloody pit" in *Historic Haunted America*. "The digging of this railroad tunnel is a saga of blood, sweat and tears. Begun in 1851, it wasn't finished until 1875. During those twenty-four years, hundreds of miners, using mostly crude black powder and pick and shovel, chipped away at the unyielding rock of Hoosac Mountain," Norman and Scott wrote. "By the time the tunnel was finished, two hundred men had lost their lives in what came to be known as 'the bloody pit.' Most died in explosions, fires, and drownings, but one death may not have been accidental."

Two men, Ned Brinkman and Billy Nash, were killed during a nitroglycerin-induced explosion on March 20, 1865. The man who prematurely set off the explosion, Ringo Kelley, managed to escape the wrath of "the bloody pit" that afternoon but one year later he mysteriously disappeared. Kelley's body was found two miles inside of the Hoosac Tunnel, at the exact spot where Brinkman and Nash had died. He'd been strangled to death. There were no suspects ... at least among the living.

How did Kelley die? Ghost lore enthusiasts claimed that Kelley was murdered by the vengeful spirits of Brinkman and Nash. Over the years, multiple sources who were brave enough to venture inside the Hoosac Tunnel claimed to see phantom miners and hear mysterious groans.

One man, Frank Webster, said he was summoned inside "the bloody pit" in 1874 by a voice in the darkness. Webster then said he saw floating apparitions. One of the apparitions supposedly grabbed Webster's rifle and hit him over the head with it. He was missing for three days and later told authorities about his close encounter in the tunnel. According to the police report, when Webster showed up, his rifle was missing and he looked like he'd seen a ghost.

Bagan's theory—that the granite boulders taken from the Hoosac Tunnel and placed on the Houghton's property somehow cursed the land—is compelling. The actual *Ghost Adventures* investigation uncovered some convincing evidence including an inexplicable mist in Mary Houghton's room. For the record, previous investigators have captured EVPs of ghostly screams and a menacing voice from beyond that commanded the investigators to "get out."

There are also photos of a ghostly face peeking out of the third-floor window. Not surprisingly, it's on the top floor where the servants, including Houghton's chauffeur Widders, once lived. Neighbors also said they've seen lights on in the third floor, which is impossible as there's no electricity on the top level.

Author Joni Mayhan has encountered a dark entity in the basement of the mansion. Her paranormal team spotted him in the form of a shadow figure moving in the darkness. *Photo by Frank C. Grace.*

Like Mayhan, Bagans encountered something paranormal in the basement of the Houghton Mansion. He captured a voice of an older man clearly saying, "ran for help." Was it Widders, Houghton's driver, professing his guilty conscience in the afterlife? It's hard to tell. There are so many layers to the multiple spirits inhabiting this extremely haunted hot spot in North Adams.

Chapter 6

JOSHUA WARD HOUSE
SALEM
MOST HAUNTED: #6

"I could feel the hand on my shoulder, weighing me down. When I turned around, nobody was there."

—JOSHUA WARD HOUSE'S FORMER PORTER

The dead love Salem. Known for its annual Halloween "Haunted Happenings" gathering, it's no surprise that the historic Massachusetts seaport is considered to be one of New England's most haunted destinations. With city officials emphasizing its not-so-dark past, tourists from all over the world seem to focus on the wicked intrigue surrounding the 1692 witch trials.

As far as the paranormal is concerned, the city is considered to be hallowed ground.

The Joshua Ward House at 148 Washington St. in Salem was purchased by Lark Hotels and was transformed into a boutique hotel called "The Merchant" in 2015. *Photo by Sam Baltrusis.*

Originally called Naumkeag, Salem means "peace." However, as its historical legacy dictates, the city was anything but peaceful during the late seventeenth century. In fact, when accused witch and landowner Giles Corey was pressed to death over a two-day period, he allegedly cursed the sheriff and the city. Over the years, his specter has allegedly been spotted preceding disasters in Salem, including the fire that destroyed most of the downtown area in June 1914. Based on my research, a majority of the hauntings conjured up in Salem over the city's tumultuous three-hundred-year-old history have ties to disaster, specifically the one-hundred-year-old fire that virtually annihilated the once prosperous North Shore seaport.

Cursed? Salem is full of secrets.

My first ghost tour experience in Salem was an impromptu trek on Mollie Stewart's Spellbound tour in 2010. I remember gazing up at the allegedly haunted Joshua Ward House and being convinced I had seen a spirit looking out of the second-floor window. It turned out to be a bust of George Washington. Soon after writing my first book, *Ghosts of Boston*, I signed on to give historical-based ghost tours of my own in a city that both excited and terrified me. I let Salem's spirits guide me.

One of my first face-to-face encounters with a negative entity was at the Joshua Ward House. I felt a warm sensation on my chest one night in September 2012 while I was giving a ghost tour. It felt like a spider bite. However, I wasn't prepared for the bitter truth. After the tour, I lifted up my shirt and noticed three cat-like scratch marks on my chest. In the paranormal world, this is called the "mark of intrinity" and it's said to signify the touch of a demonic entity. I was terrified.

After the incident, I refused to get too close to the haunted and potentially evil structure.

In 2015, the Joshua Ward House at 148 Washington St. was purchased by Lark Hotels and was transformed into a boutique hotel. Renamed "The Merchant," the posh overnight haunt celebrates Salem's rich maritime past. No mention of the reported ghosts and demonic entity allegedly lurking in the shadows of this chic new hot spot.

Are the new owners in complete denial of the structure's haunted history? Yep.

Salem somehow manages to embrace its dark, witch trial past while simultaneously shutting a door on it. The city's dualities are at war: Light versus dark. Truth versus fiction. Witches versus zombies. On the one hand, there seems to be a push to pretend that Salem's maritime past was a golden age, but in actual fact, its history is soaked in blood.

Joshua Ward was a wealthy maritime merchant and sea captain. Originally, the house had a view of the South River, but in 1830, the Front Street waterway was filled in.

"The Joshua Ward House, on Washington Street opposite Front Street, was once symbolic of Salem's early prosperity," reported the *Salem Evening News* in 1979. "When George Washington visited the city in 1789, he asked to stay at the house, then only a few years old."

For the record, the white statue peeking out of the building's second floor isn't a mysterious specter; it's a bust of our first president, commemorating his short stay in the city. Oddly, Washington opted for late October when he visited Salem. Yep, he was two hundred years too early for the city's Haunted Happenings festivities.

Listed on the National Register of Historical Places in 1978, the three-floor Federal-style building had a stint as the Washington Hotel in the late nineteenth century. It stood vacant for years and was restored in the late '70s. When Carlson Realty moved into the historic house, mysterious events started to occur. Chairs, lampshades, trashcans and candlesticks would be found turned upside down when the staff arrived in the morning. Papers were strewn on the floor, and candles were bent in the shape of an "S." One of the offices on the second floor is ice cold, a telltale sign of paranormal activity.

Why would the Joshua Ward House be haunted?

The house was built on the foundation of Sheriff George Corwin's old house, and many people believe the venerated sheriff's spirit lingers at the 148 Washington St. locale. In fact, his body was buried beneath the building but was later interred at Broad Street Cemetery.

After mysteriously dying from a heart attack at age thirty, the younger Corwin was arguably the city's most despised man and rightfully so. The then 20-something sheriff reportedly got a kick out of torturing the men and women accused of witchcraft. Although it was the uncle, Magistrate Jonathan Corwin, who tried and accused the innocents, it was the sick and twisted nephew who enforced the unjust verdicts.

"Sheriff Corwin was so disliked by the people of Salem, that when he died of a heart attack in 1696, his family didn't dare bury him in the cemetery for fear he'd be dug up and his body torn limb from limb," wrote Robert Ellis Cahill, himself a former Essex County sheriff turned author, in *Haunted Happenings*. Corwin's cruelty is legendary. For example, he sent an officer to accused witch Mary Parker's home in Andover on September 23, 1692, literally the day after her execution, demanding that her son fork over the dead woman's farm and goods. Parker's son, who was still mourning the loss of his mother, had to cough up a large sum of money to stop Corwin's demands for corn, hay and cattle.

Of course, Corwin is also known as the man who tried to squeeze a confession out of Giles Corey, the elderly landowner who was pressed to death after a torturous two-day ordeal. "Do you confess?" demanded Corwin, as his men piled more rocks on the stubborn Corey. Corwin reportedly would stand on top of the rocks as the old man demanded "more weight."

"In the crushing, Giles Corey's tongue was pressed out of his mouth and the sheriff, with his cane, forced it in again," wrote Robert Calef in his account of the torture. According to legend, Corey cursed the sheriff and Salem right before he passed. "Damn you, Sheriff," Corey allegedly cried out. "I curse you and Salem."

When Corwin died in 1696, he was a wanted man. Phillip English, a wealthy merchant who fled Salem to Boston and ultimately New York with his wife, Mary, after wrongfully being accused, supposedly threatened to place a lien on Corwin's body until his property was returned. For the record, the sheriff's cronies had ransacked English's estate and English demanded posthumous justice. Corwin was buried beneath his home at 148 Washington St. and was later moved when tempers cooled to the Broad Street Cemetery with his equally disliked uncle, Judge Jonathan Corwin.

"Employees of Higginson Book Company relay stories of a female ghost sighted upstairs in one of the rooms," confirmed the *Salem Pioneer* in 1998. "Another sighting, that of the sheriff himself, was said to have been witnessed by another former book publisher."

The oddest piece of paranormal evidence was a Polaroid photo shot at a Carlson Realty holiday party in the '80s. According to lore, Carlson shot a photo of what was originally described as a light-haired woman enjoying the holiday festivities. What came out of the camera was something entirely different. It's a haggard woman, with translucent skin and frizzy black hair.

The creepy photo made its debut in Robert Cahill's book *Ghostly Haunts* in the '80s. Producers from *Unsolved Mysteries* picked it up, had the photo checked out for its authenticity and blasted it on national TV. The picture became local legend. Truthfully, the spooky snapshot looked like it could have been the later-identified subject, Julie Tremblay, standing in front of a holiday wreath. Contrary to local lore, Tremblay had dark hair.

In addition to the picture, there are many firsthand accounts of encounters with the witchy crone spirit. Cahill's sister-in-law told the author she saw the lady in black at the Joshua Ward House. "I immediately noticed a strange-looking woman sitting in a wingback chair across the hall in another office," she claimed. "The woman's skin didn't look like flesh, but was almost transparent like glass. She looked like a mannequin, just staring into space."

Then there is the report of visitors experiencing a choking sensation in George Washington's former room on the second floor. People have attributed this spirit to Corwin because of his notoriously sadistic approach to the witch trials victims. "All the lights were out and upon entering it my throat immediately tightened up," reported Cahill's assistant. "It was like someone was choking me. I was being strangled but I didn't feel any hands around my throat. Yet I felt my throat close up."

According to Cahill's theory, this sort of poltergeist activity would make sense. He claimed that Corwin was known as "the strangler" because of "his cruel method of torture used to gain confessions." However, there is little evidence to confirm that Corwin did, in fact, strangle his victims.

Based on anecdotal evidence, the entity at the Joshua Ward House doesn't like men. It seems that women actually see the lady in black, and men are often attacked, whether it's inexplicable scratch marks on their chests or the overwhelming sensation of being choked when entering the same second-floor room.

The building's porter claimed to have been grabbed from behind by an unseen force. "I could feel the hand on my shoulder, weighing me down," he told Cahill. "When I turned around, nobody was there."

Many believe the Joshua Ward House ghost is one of the women Corwin wrongly arrested and tortured. Yes, she's seeking postmortem revenge.

Chapter 7

LONGFELLOW'S WAYSIDE INN
SUDBURY
MOST HAUNTED: #7

"We recorded crying on a device that only
records electromagnetic fields. It blew our
mind because it was someone balling."

—MICHAEL BAKER, PARA-BOSTON INVESTIGATOR

Jerusha Howe, the resident wailing spirit of Longfellow's Wayside Inn,
was known as the Belle of Sudbury. She also is said to have died in 1842
from a broken heart. Her legend, which was immortalized by the alpha-
male paranormal investigation team from the Travel Channel's *Ghost
Adventures*, has morphed over the years.

However, one story has been consistent. The ghostly woman is said to
haunt Room 9, her old bed chamber, and 10 which is believed to be where
she sewed.

For the record, Longfellow's Wayside Inn was built in 1716. Originally
called Howe Tavern, it was renamed after Henry Wadsworth Longfellow
visited the historic hot spot with his publisher James Fields in October
1862. Longfellow penned the book *Tales of a Wayside Inn* in 1863.

Jerusha was the oldest sister of the last Howe innkeeper, Lyman, who was known as "the squire" back in the 1800s. "She was well educated, she was well dressed, loved to paint and read and sing to the guests and visitors of the inn," explained former innkeeper John Cowden to WBZ-TV. "People want this room because of the history with Jerusha. Its ambiance, dark paneling and plank flooring," the innkeeper explained, adding that there's a Secret Drawer Society where guests can leave behind notes of what they experienced in Room 9.

According to Cowden, guests claim they hear Howe playing her piano and her footsteps in the night. The innkeeper told WBZ-TV that he'd never encountered the ghosts of Longfellow's Wayside Inn. "I have not experienced them myself, but because we heard so many you just don't know," he continued.

The man who ditched Howe promised to come back to Sudbury to continue their courtship but never did. Born in 1797, she died at 45, unmarried and heartbroken.

What happened to her beloved? "Little is known of Jerusha's romantic affairs in life, but as the story goes, she was engaged to an Englishman," explained Alyson Horrocks in *Yankee Magazine*. "The legend claims that he sailed home to England to make arrangements for the wedding, and was never heard from again. There has been speculation that he drowned at sea or he simply abandoned her, and perhaps he never existed at all."

According to *Ghost Adventures* frontman Zak Bagans, Jerusha is "America's most amorous female ghost" and he felt like her spirit was teasing him during the paranormal investigation or "lockdown," making Bagans want more.

"Longfellow's Wayside Inn is home to America's most romantic haunt," announced Bagans on the February 2011 Travel Channel episode. "The ghost of a woman who still pines away waiting for her lover to return from across the sea is experienced throughout the building. It is said that she only focuses on the men who sleep in her bedroom."

Longfellow's Wayside Inn in Sudbury is rumored to be haunted by the ghost of Jerusha Howe. *Photo by Frank C. Grace.*

In the episode, Bagans continued to sexualize the dead woman's post-mortem pleas for the British visitor she fell in love with in the early 1840s. Bagans jokingly surmised that "guests have had intimate encounters with Jerusha" and announced his intentions to "hook up" with the female spirit at Longfellow's Wayside Inn. "Sorry everybody to bug your Valentine's Day dinner," Bagans awkwardly said from the dinner table. "I do have something I would like to say. There's a spirit of a woman who is very beautiful. She's gorgeous and that's who I'm going to hook up with."

Bagans interviewed Dan Grillo, a regular overnight guest who stays in the notoriously haunted Room 9. Grillo said he had a face-to-face encounter with Jerusha's ghost, adding that "it wasn't sexual. It was comforting." The spirit allegedly only appears to men, even when the man's wife is sharing the bed.

"It was two in the morning," recalled Grillo. "An arm went around me and went across my back and I was like, 'who is this?' I jumped up at the side of the bed. It was a clear impression."

Was it Jerusha? "Oh yeah," Grillo responded. "Other people I've talked to say they've seen her standing in the corner."

Bagan's investigation produced some compelling evidence. He claimed to have seen a ghostly dress sway near Jerusha's room although it wasn't captured on camera. The team did film a misty form with a distinct head using a full-spectrum camera. They also experienced female cries, mysterious tapping, temperature fluctuations and doors slamming in both Room 9 and 10. Bagans claimed that Jerusha put her icy-cold hands on his knees and the spirit played with his belt. After the lockdown, Bagans spent a night alone in Howe's room to get to know her better. Fellow castmates Nick Groff and Aaron Goodwin joked that Bagans had a "ghost fetish."

Based purely on the special Valentine's Day *Ghost Adventures* episode, Howe is a sex-crazed succubus. Michael Baker, founder of the scientific group called the New England Center for the Advancement of Paranormal Science (NECAPS) and lead investigator with Para-Boston, said Bagans painted an over-the-top and somewhat misogynistic portrait of Wayside Inn's resident ghost.

Wayside Inn's Old Bar room is the oldest room in the historic structure. It was the first floor chamber of David Howe's 1707 two-room homestead and became a watering hole called Howe's Tavern in 1716 and eventually Red Horse Tavern. *Photo by Frank C. Grace.*

Howe is heartbroken over an unrequited love affair. Based on Baker's exhaustive research, she possibly left a psychic imprint from her emotional breakdown when the Englishman didn't respond to her letters.

Apparently, the cliché "hell hath no fury like a woman scorned" also applies in the afterlife.

"That *Ghost Adventures* episode is horrendous," responded Baker. "We have captured a lot of evidence at the Wayside Inn over the years. It started with a knock on the door. The entire group heard it and looked at the door and we recorded it. We opened the door right away and no one was there. The stairs outside are narrow, curved and extremely creaky. No one could have knocked on that door and got away that fast unheard."

Baker's "real science, real answers" mantra cuts through the usual smoke and mirrors associated with the "Boo!" business. With Baker, there's no over-the-top *Ghostbusters* gear or fake Cockney accents. When it comes to science-based paranormal investigations, Baker is the real deal.

"Basically, there is no ghost-catching device," explained Baker. "The field has changed. It has taken more of a fun-house approach—it has become a novelty—and it has set the paranormal investigation field back in a way. A lot of people are trying to use a screwdriver to hammer a nail. People go in with preconceived notions, and if anything happens, they're going to come to a certain conclusion. If something moves, bumps or they hear footsteps, they're going to automatically assume that it's a ghost, and that's a bad way to investigate."

Baker continued: "Technology can't detect spirits … we have to prove that spirits exist before we can build anything that can measure them. There was a shift in the field, occurring in the '90s, where it's a game to mimic what is seen on television. There was a period where it was purely scientific, and now people think they can turn off the lights, pick up an infrared camera and capture a ghost."

Baker said Longfellow's Wayside Inn is arguably the most active location he's investigated. "We recorded a video of a shadow coming out of the floor twice. The first time it came out of the floor and back down and the next time it flew over the bed. This video confirmed the location of guest sightings. Then I recorded someone fumbling on a piano at 4 a.m. It wasn't a song. It was fumbling and it lasted 20 minutes. Jerusha's piano is there but it doesn't work and is in the museum at the other end of the inn. It was audible to the ears and I couldn't hear it outside the room. Jerusha used to play that piano in her room."

The paranormal investigator said Howe's cries were captured on tape. "We recorded crying on a device that only records electromagnetic fields. It was captured in the same area as the shadow. It blew our mind because it was someone balling," he explained.

"That same night the hot water in the bathroom turned on itself. We had cameras running in the room while we ate dinner. When we returned from dinner the water in the bathroom had turned on. We could hear the water running on our recordings. We listened to the recordings when the last person used the bathroom and no water was heard. So something turned the water on full blast while we left the room. The bathroom is also in the same area as the shadow."

Baker, who normally is Para-Boston's skeptic, said he believes that Longfellow's Wayside Inn is one of the most haunted locations in Massachusetts. "I'm convinced because each time these things occurred they happened with strict controls and monitoring of the environment," Baker continued. "There was no obvious explanation and these things should not have been possible. They shouldn't have occurred but they did."

The paranormal investigator said the Wayside Inn's ghost lore extends beyond Jerusha. "There was a sighting at the end in the 1800s of a half-body woman walking through what is now the ballroom. It left such an impression that they renamed the room the Hobgoblin Room.

According to Brian E. Plumb's *A History of Longfellow's Wayside Inn*, "a woman of the Howe family [long ago] claimed she saw a ghost floating, half running through this room on a dark night." The Hobgoblin Room, once called the Old Hall, was rechristened in 1868 after the historic ghost sighting.

Baker and his team have spent months scanning and transcribing letters from the Secret Drawer Society, which chronicle encounters guests have had with Howe's ghost. A tradition dating to 1990 but believed to have started in 1923, the notes are kept in the nooks and crannies of Jerusha's room. "The best part about them is it's unsolicited testimony," concluded Baker. "Nobody asked those people if they had a paranormal experience. The experience itself moved them to write those notes."

Hundreds of letters are kept in Baker's database. One note, written on New Year's Day in 2006, talked about an encounter with Jerusha in the wee hours of the night on Jan. 1. "They say you only appear to men but both my wife and I heard you," wrote one anonymous guest. "After seeing a jagged beam of white light and hearing your strange knocking, we managed to drift back to sleep. You have made us question our beliefs in the supernatural and the structure of life. Your presence has confirmed for us that we are not alone."

Chapter 8

USS SALEM
QUINCY
MOST HAUNTED: #8

*"The most active was the captain's quarters where
we got EVPs. The men didn't like ladies on their
ship. I think the ghosts of the men who served
still reside with their old-school rules."*

—RACHEL HOFFMAN, PARANORMAL XPEDITIONS

Launched on March 25, 1947, in Fore River Shipyard in Quincy and nicknamed "The Sea Witch" by her crew thanks to a three-month stint in the so-called witch city, the *USS Salem* never saw combat but was certainly a harbinger of death. In fact, her mess hall became a makeshift morgue during an earthquake off the coast of Greece in 1953 and it's estimated that at least 400 dead bodies were kept on the vessel. According to additional reports, at least 23 babies were born on the ship during the 1950s.

"The *USS Salem CA-139* has been coined 'the haunted ship' after its share of deaths," reported Lana Law in *Haunted* Sites *in North America*. "For instance, during the 1953 Ionian Earthquake the *USS Salem CA-139* served as a hospital ship. As a result, it has been reputed to have hauntings."

The *USS Salem* is moving from its homebase at the Fore River Shipyard in Quincy to an undetermined location. *Photo by Frank C. Grace.*

Rachel Hoffman, an investigator with Paranormal Xpeditions and a frequent visitor to the ghost ship, said her team uncovered a lot of activity in the third mess hall, which is where the bodies were kept during the earthquake. "We heard a crying baby in the medical area," she said, adding that there are tables with stirrups indicating facilities for childbirth. "The meat locker where the bodies were kept while at sea was the thickest, most active area," Hoffman said, adding that her team heard banging and that others reported being touched when no one else was on board.

The *USS Salem*, moving from her home in Quincy to an undetermined location, also boasts a few misogynistic spirits who frequently retaliated when Hoffman's all-female crew investigated the ship. For the record, the vessel was decommissioned in 1959 and its alleged spirits reflect the sentiment prevalent during the World War II era. "The most active was the captain's quarters where we got EVPs," she continued. "The men didn't like ladies on their ship. I think the ghosts of the men who served still reside with their old-school rules." Paranormal Xpeditions also picked up an EVP of what sounded like a pig on the top deck.

Michael Condon, the *USS Salem*'s executive director, told *Metrowest Daily* that multiple people have reported seeing a ghost-like figure lurking near the machinery on the vessel's bow. "I'm just going to say this: While I have not seen anything, I certainly have heard things," he said. "What for us was a neat little secret we had—that there were ghosts on this ship—has turned into something that is not our little secret anymore."

The *USS Salem*'s proverbial ghost cat was let out of the bag in October 2009 when Syfy's *Ghost Hunters* investigated the 718-foot battleship.

In the anchor windlass room, Condon told the The Atlantic Paranormal Society team that "one of our volunteers, his name was John, used to work in this space, maintaining and cleaning it. One day he passed away and we noticed people saying they met this terrific tour guide named John," Condon said, adding that they didn't have any tour guides on the ship at that time. "He's very active in this spot and people actively see him and even talk to him."

Tom Ventosi, a volunteer with the *USS Salem*, said he saw a woman in white in the restricted medical area. "As I looked down the hall, you could see a woman taking a right. She was in white shorts, white shirt and had a white handbag. She just turned and walked. And when we went down there and looked where she went there was only a metal wall. We couldn't find her anywhere."

Condon mentioned that he's heard an EVP of a woman in the medical area, near the tables with stirrups, saying "get out, get out." However, Condon said the agitated spirit could be saying "get it out" which could be a reference to the multiple children born on the *USS Salem*.

The executive director also told TAPS that he spotted a shadow figure in the machine shop. The ship's archivist, John Connors, said he's heard phantom footsteps above him when he's working. "It's always right above my head," Connors explained. "I go up on the main deck to see if there are any cars in the parking lot and there are no cars there, except my truck. I look around to see if anybody is onboard … nobody."

Paranormal Xpedition's Rachel Hoffman has heard a crying baby in the medical area. The tables with stirrups were used as facilities for childbirth. *Photo by Frank C. Grace.*

The *Ghost Hunters* crew did pick up footsteps immediately and claimed to have heard a woman's voice. Grant Wilson said he saw a shadowy black figure creep up the gangplank. They also picked up high levels of electromagnetic activity which could result in uneasy feelings of paranoia.

During the reveal, they picked up a low-grade EVP and other inexplicable bumps in the night. "What does it come down to? We have some bangs that we can't explain and we have some low, subtle voices," said Wilson, mentioning his close encounter with the shadow figure.

"I truly believe there is something going on here," Jason Hawes confirmed. "I would like to come back and investigate."

If *Ghost Hunters* does return, the *USS Salem* will be docked in a different location. It's slotted to move to Boston Harbor Shipyard and Marina next to the Nantucket Lightship in East Boston. "However, the location is not confirmed."

In 2013, access to the vessel was shut down because the MBTA deemed the wharf at its homebase was unstable. Before its move to an undetermined location, the ship had a 20-year run as the U.S. Naval Shipbuilding Museum in Quincy and served as a symbol of the city's shipbuilding history during the 1940s. "We love Quincy and we felt that Quincy was the reason why the ship existed as a museum," Condon told the *Patriot Ledger*. "But in the end, we felt the East Boston location is a place where the museum can blossom."

Is the *USS Salem* haunted? Absolutely. However, it's my belief that the ghosts of the aged battleship are, for the most part, a psychic imprint from its Cold War-era heydey.

For the record, a residual haunting isn't technically a ghost but a playback or recording of a past event. Based on the so-called Stone Tape theory, apparitions aren't intelligent spirits that interact with the living but psychic imprints that happen especially during moments of high tension, such as childbirth, a murder or during intense moments of a person's life. According to the hypothesis, residual hauntings are simply non-interactive playbacks, similar to a movie.

Speaking of the silver screen, the *USS Salem* made a cameo in the action-packed thriller from Disney called *The Finest Hours* starring Casey Affleck and Chris Pine. The vessel was also featured in a film called the *Pursuit of the Graf Spee* in 1956.

Next stop: *Ghost Ship II?*

Chapter 9

SPIDER GATES CEMETERY
LEICESTER
MOST HAUNTED: #9

*"The whole interaction was just spooky.
The two came out of nowhere."*

—LIZ TAEGEL, *"13 MOST HAUNTED" VIDEOGRAPHER*

There are so many myths swirling around the Quaker burial ground, called Friends Cemetery, in Leicester, I didn't know what to expect when I visited. Also known as Spider Gates Cemetery because of the mysterious cobweb-style iron gates welcoming visitors to this allegedly haunted hot spot, its eerie vibe is punctuated by its off-the-beaten path location tucked away near the Worcester airport.

My first impression of this so-called eighth gate to hell? It's nearly impossible to find using a GPS-driven navigation system. Luckily, veteran paranormal photographer Frank C. Grace intuitively knew where to go on Manville Street and my team, including videographer Liz Taegel from the *13 Most Haunted* TV show, meandered down a mosquito-infested path with a yellow gate.

#9

The hanging tree where a teen allegedly was hanged at the Friends Cemetery, also known as Spider Gates, in Leicester. *Photo by Frank C. Grace.*

I quickly walked through the marsh to the wrought-iron fence I've heard about for years. It was an oddly foreboding journey back in time. The hanging tree to the left of the wrought-iron fence, where a teen boy is said to have been hanged in the 1980s, served as an eerie sentinel warning visitors of the horrors rumored to have unfolded in this beautifully landscaped Friends Cemetery.

For the record, there is only one gate and not eight. However, this is just the tip of the iceberg regarding the misinformation surrounding this cemetery chock-full of urban legends.

Other Spider Gates stories suggest that there's another cemetery nearby that can only be found once. White ectoplasm supposedly oozes from the ground and the rocks outside of the cemetery wall have runes etched in them. All not true.

But is Spider Gates haunted? Sometimes fact is stranger than fiction.

Taegel, who was lagging behind the team, was filming the trek through the woods and somehow dropped her car keys in the grass. A man, who Taegel described as a skeletal-looking figure accompanied by a female companion came out of nowhere and returned her keys. The gatekeeper's voice was so loud it boomed 50 feet or so to the cemetery. "You dropped your keys ma'am," he said. Taegel recalled later that the gatekeeper enunciated his words with an old-school New England accent. She said his voice sounded like a turn-of-the-century throwback to another era.

The videographer's complexion turned a ghostly white after she interacted with the man and his friend. As soon as Taegel retrieved her keys, the mysterious duo walked into the marshland, which had no clear path, and the videographer said they were gone in a flash.

"The whole interaction was just spooky," mused Taegel in hindsight. "The two came out of nowhere."

Local ghost-lore enthusiast Christine Broderick said she also had a close encounter near the stream where Taegel met the cemetery's gatekeeper. "We went a few years ago to Spider Gates and walked around near the stream," she recalled. "I was alone and my friends were up ahead. I swear it sounded like something was rushing down the woods straight toward me. I thought it was one of my friends trying to scare me. They were running fast so I screamed like a little girl and ran and caught up with my friends."

Broderick continued: "It wasn't them. So they all came back with me and right where I first heard the noise like someone running through the woods a huge tree had fallen and that was definitely not the noise I heard. I thanked the ghosts or whatever because I would be under that tree."

Once entering the so-called eighth gate to hell, visitors are greeted with the cemetery's alleged hanging tree to the left. According to lore, a local teenage boy tied a noose around his neck and somehow jumped from the tree in the 1980s. His spirit is said to follow people around and some claim to have felt the boy tug at their shirt or worse—grab unexpected guests around the neck.

Believed to be the eighth gate to hell, Spider Gates Cemetery earned its nickname because of the mysterious cobweb-style iron gates welcoming curiosity seekers. *Photo by Frank C. Grace.*

There are no reported hangings at Friends Cemetery. However, there may actually be a sliver of truth to the tall tale. According to Daniel V.

Boudillion, there was a rumored apparent suicide on Manville Road, which is connected to the cemetery by a dirt path. "There was a hanging in the '70s in the area on Manville Street heading toward Paxton Street near the reservoir on the left side," recalled Boudillion on his website. "A mother and daughter were out picking pinecones and found him. I don't remember his name but it was in the paper. He was a local boy and they found him with his hands and feet bound hanging from a tree."

Boudillion also included a picture of what looks like a full-bodied apparition of a boy sitting on the tree. He's greenish in color and seems to be wearing a school uniform. He's called "green boy" and the color is significant in the paranormal realm. It represents nature and the heart. According to paranormal researchers, green symbolizes a spirit that once walked the Earth. So, if it is in fact a ghost, he's earthbound.

Walking past the creepy hanging tree, you can see a spot in the center that people claim was used as a satanic "altar" in black mass rituals and ceremonial sacrifices. The raised area is where the Quaker meetinghouse originally stood. So, the plateau stone posts marking each corner is formerly a foundation. This doesn't rule out the possibility of ritualistic gatherings, especially during the '60s and '70s.

However, the actual location was formerly a spiritual homebase to the Quaker families buried at the Friends Cemetery. The oldest gravestones date back to the 1700s and the most recent burial was in 2000. In other words, it's an active burial ground in more ways than one.

The series of gravestones to the left of the supposed evil altar marks the final resting place of the Earle family. The grave on the far left belongs to Marmaduke Earle, who is the focus of a Spider Gates urban legend. "If you walk around Marmaduke's gravestone 10 times at midnight and say 'Marmaduke speak to me,' kneel down and put your head on the gravestone and listen, he would speak to you," Bourdillion's source reported. "I have been there at night and I can say that you could hear groans of some sort but there is a house on Manville Street before the dirt road and the people who lived there are the Grangers. They had cows and when they moo it could sound like groans and moans."

According to a Spider Gates Cemetery urban legend, if you walk around Marmaduke Earle's gravestone 10 times and ask he him to speak, he will. *Photo by Frank C. Grace.*

The cemetery is also close to the Worcester airport. While taping our *13 Most Haunted* documentary, we heard several planes fly overhead and the noise emanated throughout the cemetery.

The nearby airport may be the culprit for another Spider Gates mystery. Visitors report hearing a roar from the wooded area behind the cemetery. Our video team headed into the area and oddly, the batteries to our video camera mysteriously drained. Once we left the spot, the equipment returned to normal.

One woman ventured out to the wooded place where our batteries had drained. "I'll never go back there again," claimed an anonymous source. "I was walking my dog in the area and came upon the cemetery. While I was checking out some of the stones, my dog ran deeper into the cemetery and disappeared near the altar area. I soon heard barking, a yelp and then nothing. When I went looking for him, I found blood everywhere and then nothing. There were no animal tracks around, but there was a horrible smell of sulfur."

The source said Spider Gates is home to a demonic entity. "I never went back," she continued. "The place is truly evil."

Another blogger talked about a horrific experience one night in 1991. "Some stuff happened with my friend," he said. "I chased her into the actual cemetery. Something grabbed me by the arm and threw me down. After that I don't remember but I have the scars on my arm to prove it and they aren't human."

While exploring the wooded area, my team searched for a laid-stone culvert or Shaker-style cave that's believed to be where a young girl was murdered and mutilated. Based on historical research, the story of the female isn't true. However, there was a horrific death involving a six-year-old boy from the Mcauley Nazareth Home for Boys on Mulberry Street. According to reports, he was pummeled to death by a 16-year-old classmate and dumped in Lynde Brook, which is less than one mile from Spider Gates.

The photo of the "green boy" taken from the supposed hanging tree fits the description of the murdered six-year-old student. Could the Spider

Gates haunting be tied to the Nazareth student and not the unsubstantiated hanging? Yes, it's possible. When it comes to the Friends Cemetery in Leiceister, the "green boy" story is only one of a handful of yarns local thrillseekers have weaved.

Chapter 10

BOSTON LIGHT
LITTLE BREWSTER ISLAND
MOST HAUNTED: #10

"I won't say if I believe or don't believe in any ghosts on the island. Let's just say I've heard plenty of stories. Some strange things do happen out here."

—SALLY SNOWMAN, BOSTON LIGHT'S LIGHTKEEPER

"Something touched me in there and it wasn't human," screamed a girl running out of the corridor of dungeons after a field trip to Fort Warren at Georges Island. "It was the Lady in Black."

She looked mortified. During the summer of 2014, I gave historical tours with Boston Harbor Cruises and traveled on large vessels carrying passengers back and forth from Georges Island. I spent most afternoons during the summer searching for a repeat experience with a shadow figure I had seven years prior. No luck.

#10

Boston Light nestled on the Harbor's Little Brewster Island is celebrating its 300-year anniversary in 2016. *Photo by Frank C. Grace.*

In 2007, I moved back to Boston and had a moment while touring the ramparts of Fort Warren at Georges Island. Out of the corner of my eye, I noticed an all-black shadow figure. I looked again, and it was gone. At this point, I had never heard of the Lady in Black legend. I just intuitively knew Georges Island had some sort of psychic residue. While researching Fort Warren's back story, my interest in Boston's haunted past slowly started to become a passion. History repeats itself, and it was my job to uncover the truth and give a voice to those without a voice—even though most of the stories turned out to be tales from the crypt.

Lawrence, a fellow Boston Harbor Cruises tour guide and former park ranger, insisted that Georges Island wasn't inhabited by ghosts, adding that the Lady in Black legend was completely made up by folklorist Edward R. Snow. "I spent so many nights there, I would know," he said while we were passing Nix's Mate en route to the mainland. "However, I would say the island has a spirit. Some rangers say the island's energy, or spirit, welcomes people."

In hindsight, I've decided that my encounter on Georges in 2007 was the island's spirit welcoming me to the island. However, there are ghosts nearby.

While several of the 34 islands have alleged paranormal activity, Boston Harbor's most haunted island is surely Little Brewster Island—in particular, the Boston Light that stands on it. It's located behind Georges Island and can be spotted from the ramparts I explored regularly during the summer of 2014. While I was giving historical tours, the lighthouse was closed for much-needed repairs in preparation for its 300-year anniversary.

When Boston Light reopened in 2015, the island once again became a Boston Harbor hot spot.

"Over the past four centuries, dozens of islands that dot Boston Harbor have seen plundering pirates run aground, major battles won and lost, prisoners confined, and thousands felled by war and disease," wrote George Steitz in *Haunted Lighthouses*. He added that the body of water surrounding the "beacon upon a hill" is arguably America's most historic and, perhaps, most haunted. "The aftermath may have left the surrounding waters brimming with restless spirits."

Yes, there are ghosts lurking in the waters near the Hub's historic seaport and inhabiting a handful of the 34 secluded islands scattered throughout Boston Harbor.

Since 1716, ships have passed one of the oldest lighthouses in America, the Boston Light, which stands as an eerie sentinel, guarding the secrets of the mainland's dark past. "I think people do feel a presence of spirits out there," said Holly Richardson, an officer of the Metropolitan District Commission, en route via ferry to the site of the lighthouse on Little Brewster Island. "It's a magical feeling. It's a place for one's imagination to wander." According to Steitz, hundreds of sudden, tragic deaths have occurred in the murky waters surrounding the historic lighthouse. Rick Himelrich, who worked with the U.S. Coast Guard, talked to Steitz about a ghost sighting that occurred decades ago near the Boston Light's living quarters: "The figure of a woman walked right by them. Plain as day. There were two gentlemen sitting there and they both saw her. She walked right by them." The odd thing? There were no women at the lighthouse that day. At least "not one who was a living, breathing human," the officer added.

Himelrich's tale is one of several accounts of wailing female specters and seafaring shadow figures reported to haunt the famed Boston Harbor Islands. There's the more notorious Lady in Black apparition who has been spotted creeping along the ramparts of Fort Warren on Georges Island since the Civil War. On January 18, 1644, a crew of three sailors watched in awe as a strange set of lights emerged from the chilly waters and transformed into the shape of a man near what was Governor's Island, currently an extension of Boston's Logan Airport. On Nix's Mate, one of the harbor's smallest islands, there are reports of a salty-dog specter known as William Fly, who was executed in the 1700s and hanged by the noose, which he is said to have tied himself. Sailors who pass by the tiny, off-limits Nix's Mate claim to hear blood-curdling screams and maniacal laughs from the island, which was once used as a makeshift prison and burial ground.

There's a something-wicked-this-way-comes mystique radiating from Little Brewster's Boston Light, which is approximately nine miles off-shore from downtown and dates back to 1716. It was rebuilt in the eighteenth century after the redcoats torched the original structure during the Revolutionary War. It's the second-oldest working lighthouse in the country, and its ninety-eight-foot-high tower has seen almost three centuries of tragedy, starting with the death of the light's first keeper, George Worthylake, who drowned alongside his wife, daughter and two other men when their boat capsized a few feet from the island's rocky terrain in 1718.

The ghosts from the Boston Light's early days have captivated the imagination of the city's land-bound inhabitants for years. A young Benjamin Franklin, then an up-and-coming printer, penned a ballad about the Worthylake incident called "Lighthouse Tragedy," which he later dismissed as "wretched stuff" but joked that it "sold prodigiously." Boston Light's second keeper, Robert Saunders, met a similar fate and drowned only a few days after taking the job.

The tower, which originally stood at seventy-five feet high, caught fire in 1751, and the building was damaged so intensely that only the walls remained. The British, angry that the colonists tried to disengage the beacon during the Revolution, apparently destroyed Boston Light in 1776 while heading out of the Boston Harbor. It was rebuilt in 1783 but witnessed several more tragedies, including two shipwrecks, the *Miranda* in 1861 and the *Calvin F. Baker* in 1898, which resulted in three crewmen freezing to death in the rigging. In addition to the onslaught of natural disaster, one keeper in 1844 set up a "Spanish" cigar factory, carting in young girls from Boston and claiming that the stogies sold in the city were foreign imports. Captain Tobias Cook's clandestine cigar business was quickly fingered as fraudulent and shut down.

President John F. Kennedy legislated that the Boston Light would be the last manned lighthouse in the country. It has been inhabited for almost three centuries, even when the tower was automated in 1998. One island mystery, known as the Ghost Walk, refers to a stretch of water several miles east of the lighthouse where the warning sounds from the tower's larger-than-life foghorn cannot be heard by passing ships. For years, no one has been able to scientifically explain the so-called Ghost Walk's absence of sound, not even a crew of MIT students sent in the mid-1970s to spend an entire summer on the island but who were still unable to crack the case.

However, talk of the paranormal has trumped the island's Ghost Walk mystery. "It has withstood blizzards, erosion, fires, lightning, shipwrecks and ghosts," mused a report in the April 29, 1999 edition of the *Boston Globe* that profiled Little Brewster's Chris Sutherland from the U.S. Coast Guard. Apparently, the petty officer noticed tiny human footprints in the snow while keeping the light in the late '90s. "I'm not saying it's a ghost," he said, "but I don't know. In the past, there were kids out here, lightkeepers' families. There were shipwrecks along the rocks."

A former Coast Guard engineer who lived on the island in the late '80s, David Sandrelli, told the *Globe* that there have been reports of a lady walking down the stairs. Also, he said that crew members stationed on Little Brewster would hear weird noises in the night but would dismiss them, saying, "It's just George," an allusion to the ghosts from the Worthylake tragedy.

Sally Snowman, who was the first female keeper at the last occupied lighthouse in the country, told the *Globe* in 2003 that she encountered a few "just George" moments during her stint on Little Brewster. "I won't say if I believe or don't believe in any ghosts on the island," she said. "Let's just say I've heard plenty of stories. Some strange things do happen out here, like the fog signal, which works on reading moisture in the air, going off at 3:00 a.m. on a star-filled night. That's fun because you have to walk across the island to shut that sucker off. That can be weird."

Little Brewster's mascot black Labrador, Sammy, reportedly had a close encounter in 1999. "He would stand up, run out of the room for no reason and was shaking all over," recalled a former keeper, Gary Fleming. "It really does get spooky. You have plenty of time here, and if you let your mind go, you can freak yourself out," Fleming said, adding that he believes in the supernatural.

Snowman echoed Fleming's comments about the canine mascot's odd nightly ritual. "He's been out here six years, and at dusk every night he barks and barks," she mused. "We call it the Shadwell Hour, after the slave who died."

So who's Shadwell? Mazzie B. Anderson, a woman who was stationed with her husband on Little Brewster in 1947, recalled hearing footsteps when no one was there and watching the foghorn engines magically start themselves when her husband was ill. She also heard maniacal laughter followed by the sobs of a female voice yelling, "Shaaaadwell, Shaaaadwell!" It turns out that Worthylake, his wife and their youngest daughter capsized near the island, and the oldest daughter, who was left behind with her friend Mary Thompson, sent out a rescue party, which included an African American slave, to save her drowning family. "Somehow the canoe capsized and all went overboard," wrote Anderson in the October 1998 edition of *Yankee* magazine. "The African made a valiant attempt to save all hands, but failed. The young girl was the last to go under, still calling his name. No one survived."

The name of the courageous slave? He was known as Shadwell.

Chapter 11

WITCH HOUSE
SALEM
MOST HAUNTED: #11

If it's true that "what goes around comes around," Salem has endured more than three hundred years of torturous penance. Yes, lingering negativity associated with the city's Puritan forefathers continues to affect the city. "If you look at Salem's history, it has an amazing tradition of bad karma," explained historian Tim Maguire. "The wealthy of Salem made their blood money as privateers during the Revolution. Our history is tarnished with bad events and bad karma. I feel like the energy here is more negative than it is in other places. The witches in Salem call it the spirit of place."

When it comes to curses, a bulk of Salem's bad mojo can be traced back to 1692. There are two famous legends linked to the witch trial era that continue to haunt the city. First, there are the words supposedly uttered by Giles Corey, who was pressed to death over a two-day period. Before taking his last breath, he told the sadistic sheriff George Corwin, "I curse you and Salem." According to lore, Corey's spirit appears when tragedy is about to strike. In fact, several people claimed that the "old wizard," words used by author Nathaniel Hawthorne, appeared to several locals right before the great Salem fire of 1914.

Then there is the famous hex unleashed by Sarah Good, a thirty-eight-year-old, pipe-smoking vagabond who was executed as a witch on July 19, 1692. The object of her scorn? Reverend Nicholas Noyes. He was the assistant minister at First Church and lived on Washington Street just opposite accused Bridget Bishop's house. Noyes was actively involved in the prosecution of many of the alleged witches and is known for calling the eight innocent victims dangling in Gallows Hill "firebrands of hell."

According to accounts, Reverend Noyes demanded a confession from Good, and Good, with a noose around her neck, called him a liar. "I am no more a witch than you are a wizard," she said. "And if you take away my life, God will give you blood to drink." Good had no way of knowing at the time that her words would come true, but ironically, Noyes did suffer from an aneurysm that caused blood to pour into his throat and out of his mouth. He literally choked to death on his own blood twenty-five years after Good was executed.

Salem homeboy Hawthorne alluded to Good's curse in his classic *The House of the Seven Gables*. In the book, witch trial character Matthew Maule curses his accuser, Colonel Pyncheon. Although historical record suggested that Good spewed her last words at Noyes, Hawthorne believed the venom was directed at his great-great-grandfather Judge John Hathorne.

Salem's most cursed location? It's magistrate Jonathan Corwin's former home, also known as the Witch House. My assistant and I met with the director, Elizabeth Peterson, and walked around the only standing structure from the seventeenth century. Trekking up the building's creaky stairs, it felt like we were stepping back in time. I swore I heard my name whispered on the first floor of the hallowed structure. The disembodied voice sounded female. My research assistant, a die-hard myth buster, regularly served up a healthy dose of skepticism while we explored the magical underbelly of Salem. He thinks it was merely the power of suggestion. I still don't believe him.

Salem's most haunted? Perhaps. The witch city's most historic? Absolutely.

It's the last structure standing in Salem with direct ties to the witch trial hysteria of 1692. Home of judge Jonathan Corwin, a magistrate with the Court of Oyer and Terminer, which sent nineteen to the gallows, the so-called Witch House dates back to 1675 and is an icon of America's tortured past.

Former home of Magistrate Jonathan Corwin from the 1692 witch trials, the Witch House is located at 310 Essex St. in Salem. *Photo by Sam Baltrusis.*

Paranormal investigators consider the seventeenth-century structure hallowed ground. In fact, teams including Spirit Finders Paranormal Investigators from Rhode Island fought to set up ghost-hunting equipment in the old-school building. "We're hoping to see if Judge Jonathan Corwin still resides there," said investigator Christopher Andrews in a 2008 *Boston Globe* article. "We have heard rumors of people seeing an old man sitting in one of the rooms."

Access to the house was denied. Members from the Park and Recreation Commission thought it would be in poor taste to investigate the Corwin dwelling. "We have to have respect for the gravity of the injustice that occurred in 1692," responded board member Chris Burke. "This is sort of a touchy subject," said Elizabeth Peterson, director of the house. "We want people to be aware that we're not a Salem witch attraction."

In 2011, the governing board apparently changed their minds and allowed the crew from the Travel Channel's *Ghost Adventures* to set up an overnight lockdown. When Zak Bagans, Aaron Goodwin and Nick Groff walked into the Witch House, all hell broke loose.

"In broad daylight with [Witch House director] Elizabeth Peterson and talking to her, things got really weird," Groff told the *Boston Herald*. "Zak was filming and the batteries on his wireless mike kept dying. There was some sort of energy causing his batteries to die. We felt something weird, felt cold and then the batteries died."

Groff's team fought for years to gain access to the historic property. "We've already captured a voice and we just stepped into the house to start talking about history," Groff continued. "I think we're going to be in for a long night of finding paranormal activity."

The crew supposedly picked up a child humming and an EVP of Bridget Bishop, who named "Mary" as her accuser. She kept repeating the word "apple." In Christian Day's *The Witches' Book of the Dead*, he claimed to have summoned Bishop's spirit away from her usual post at the Lyceum. "I didn't want anyone living or dead to steal the spotlight from the Witch House," he wrote. "The team mentioned recording some strong activity on the second floor, but their machines really started to get going once we arrived. Real Witches are magnets for the dead," he said, adding that he performed a necromantic blessing in the house, which included a blood offering.

Groff, in a later interview with *13 Most Haunted*, said the lockdown was a historical goldmine. "The location, the Witch House, is just absolutely awesome. To be able to walk back in time, regardless of the paranormal activity that's actually occurring there, it's just cool to step foot on those wood floors and experience the environment of what it could have been like," he said. "You're almost stepping back in time. Whatever paranormal stuff that happens there is a plus to me. It's a cool place."

In hindsight, Peterson said she has mixed feelings about the investigation. "Personally, I was very uncomfortable doing it. I love this sort of thing, so it wasn't the subject matter," Peterson told me. "They were lovely kids, but I don't think they were a good match for the house. When they were off camera, they were very different. When their camera started running out of batteries, they did pick up a child humming. My first response was shock. My second, as a mother, is that it saddens me that there may be a child's spirit here that I wasn't sensitive to or was unaware of in the house."

Peterson believes the EVP captured on *Ghost Adventures* was questionable. However, she's not saying the Witch House is free of residual energy. "There were eleven deaths in this house up until 1719," she said. "Enormous amounts of human drama unfolded in these rooms. My son thinks he's seen things, and I think I've heard things."

As far as hauntings are concerned, visitors claim to hear phantom footsteps upstairs and eerie whispers throughout the structure. Employees reported seeing inexplicable shadows in the upper floors. Psychics believe there's an angry male energy lingering in the first floor and the residual haunting of two females, one believed to be a servant trying to hide an illegitimate pregnancy.

"There's nothing malevolent here," said one Witch House tour guide. "It's subtle things. Sometimes we'll think we hear footsteps above us in the attic when nobody is in the house. A tour guide and myself were setting up for a night event, the door was locked and we did hear a shuffle in the attic. A couple of people have maintained they heard their name called when nobody else was here."

Lara Jay, another tour guide with the Witch House, confirmed the reports of paranormal activity on the History Channel 2's *Haunted History* documentary. According to her televised interview, Jay was going over a list with two visitors of those executed during the witch trials. She witnessed a tin sconce literally fly off the wall. Jay also encountered what paranormal experts call a "shadow person" in the Witch House's attic. "I saw a shadow pass on the other side of the door. I went in the room, and no one was there," Jay said. "I couldn't grasp that what I saw wasn't a living human being walking through the door … that it wasn't a human shadow."

Chapter 12

VICTORIA HOUSE
PROVINCETOWN
MOST HAUNTED: #12

"Tony Costa digs girls."

—GRAFFITI SPOTTED AT A TRURO LAUNDROMAT
DURING TONY *"CHOP CHOP"* COSTA'S TRIAL

I spent the night at what turned out to be Provincetown's murder house. I was on assignment for a magazine and booked a weekend at the Victoria House on Standish Street. I was put into Room 4 and spent the night under my covers because I heard what sounded like muted cries or a whimper coming from a boarded-up closet. The following morning, I asked to be moved out of the spooky room. I intuitively knew something horrible happened there.

Years later I found out that the Victoria House had a dark secret. Back in the 1960s, the B&B was a guest house and was home to serial killer Tony "Chop Chop" Costa. He was convicted in 1970 of two of the four murders of young women he allegedly slaughtered including Patricia H. Walsh and Mary Ann Wysocki. The house for a brief period was often pointed out to tourists as the site where the murderer lived. Costa met his victims there before luring them to his "secret garden" of marijuana before murdering and mutilating them in Truro.

According to the July 25, 1969 article in *Life* magazine penned by *Slaughterhouse-Five* author Kurt Vonnegut, Jr., Costa's room at the Standish

Street haunt was significant. "In his closet in the rooming house where he helped Patricia Walsh and Mary Ann Wysocki with their luggage, police found a coil of stained rope," Vonnegut wrote.

Guests at Provincetown's Victoria House, located at 5 Standish St., reported "uneasy feelings in the middle of the night accompanied with the smell of blood," Provincetown Paranormal Research Society posted. "Apparently it was once the home to a doctor or butcher?"

Oddly, Victoria House was the residence of the town's butcher, who cut up people not livestock. His name was Tony "Chop Chop" Costa.

The Victoria House bed and breakfast's name is a bit misleading. "I thought the house was Victorian, thus the name. But it was a misnomer as the house is definitely not Victorian," said the former owner who purchased it in 1972.

Every major city has one: a murder house. In Provincetown, it's known as the Victoria House.

Once owned by Provincetown's sheriff, the house was turned into a guest house in the 1960s, and the infamous serial killer Tony Costa stayed in what is now Room 4. Antone Charles Costa, known by the locals as Tony "Chop Chop" Costa, was convicted in 1970 of two of the four murders of young women he's believed to be responsible for: those of Patricia H. Walsh and Mary Ann Wysocki. The house for a brief period was often pointed out to tourists as the site where the murderer lived. Also, sand from the gruesome grave site was sold to gawkers for half a buck.

The Provincetown-based Costa, who was a carpenter, met his two confirmed victims at the building then called the Guest House.

Costa's crimes were particularly gruesome. When the bodies were discovered, the hearts were missing and could not be found in the graves. Each corpse was cut into parts. While the discovery of the victims caused a sensation, it was apparently the district attorney Edmund Dinis's description of the remains that caused the initial uproar. "The hearts of each girl had been removed from the bodies and were not in the graves, nor were they found," Dinis announced. "A razor like device was found near the graves. Each body was cut into as many parts as there are joints." Teeth marks were also found on the bodies.

Serial killer Tony "Chop Chop" Costa met his victims at the
structure currently called the Victoria House, located at 5
Standish St., in Provincetown. *Photo by Sam Baltrusis.*

When Kurt Vonnegut, Jr. discussed the case in *Life* magazine on July 25, 1969, the story became a national sensation. "Jack the Ripper used to get compliments about the way he dissected the women he killed," wrote Vonnegut. "Now Cape Cod has a mutilator. The pieces of four young women were found in a shallow grave. Whoever did it was no artist with the knife. He chopped up the women with what the police guess was a brush hook or an ax. It couldn't have taken too long to do."

Vonnegut talked about some "stained rope" that was found at the scene. The evidence was similar to the bloody coil found in Costa's closet in his room at 5 Standish St. The author also captured the vibe of Provincetown in this well-crafted story, mentioning telling observations including graffiti painted on a Truro laundromat: "Tony Costa digs girls."

He also poked fun at the thrillseekers. "When the bodies were found last winter, tourists arrived off-season," he wrote. "They wanted to help dig. They were puzzled when park rangers and police and firemen found them disgusting."

The story almost became the crime of the century. However, Charlie Manson's "Helter Skelter" murder spree in California trumped Costa's chopping frenzy. The "secret garden" killer was sentenced to life in prison and ended up committing suicide by hanging himself in his cell on May 12, 1974.

As far as hauntings are concerned, there have been reports of residual energy in Room 4. According to a former manager at the Victoria House, he would hear disembodied whispers throughout the guest house and the occasional scream of a female voice emanating from Room 4. Some believe that Costa may have kept his victims in the Victoria House, similar to Buffalo Bill in Silence of the Lambs, before murdering them, removing their hearts and burying them in Truro.

"In the guest house on Standish Street, near the center of town, the slain girls checked in for a night last January," the *Life* piece explained. "At the time, Tony Costa was renting a room there by the week. He was introduced to the other guests by the landlady, Mrs. Patricia Morton."

The girls checked in but they never checked out.

Jeffrey Doucette from Haunted Ptown said the stories involving Provincetown's "very own serial killer" was an unexpected point of interest. "On one tour I had just told my group that no one would jump out and frighten them," he recalled. "Boy, was I wrong. As I was about to talk about the Victoria House, I stepped into the street and there lying between two parked cars was a young man who was lying down wearing a black cloak. I let out a yelp as this was a total surprise to me. The young man realized he had startled me and some others on the tour, apologized to the group and walked away. Everyone on the tour said, 'OK that was weird.'"

Doucette said several locals came up to him, including legendary *Serial Mom* director and author John Waters, to share stories involving Tony "Chop Chop" Costa. "The famous filmmaker informed me that Mink Stole had gone on a date with Tony Costa," Doucette mused. "Luckily, she made it back without any problems."

Chapter 13

BOSTON COMMON
DOWNTOWN BOSTON
MOST HAUNTED: #13

*"Our history has many skeletons in its closet,
and the spirits want their story to be told. I'm
giving a voice to those without a voice."*

—JEFFREY DOUCETTE, *VETERAN TOUR GUIDE*

"There are bodies everywhere," I said during a taping of the Bio Channel show *Haunted Encounters: Face To Face* in 2012. "The spot where he had the initial encounter was a mass gravesite."

I was standing in front of Boylston and Tremont, an area I've identified as Boston's haunted corridor thanks to an aura of disaster imprinted by the gas-line explosion of 1897. My face-to-face encounter was with a teen spirit I now call Mary.

While writing my first book *Ghosts of Boston: Haunts of the Hub*, I started spending hours in the Boston Common. I've always felt a strong magnetic pull to the site of the Great Elm, also known as the hanging tree. I had an inexplicable interest in the Central Burying Ground, and one night while walking by the old cemetery, I noticed a young female figure wearing what looked like a hospital gown and standing by a tree. I looked back and she was gone. At this point, I didn't know about the Matthew Rutger legend dating back to the 1970s. Like me, he saw a ghost at the old cemetery. Somehow, I felt her pain.

#13

Boston-born author Edgar Allan Poe was honored with a commemorative statue on the corner of Boylston Street across from the Boston Common. *Photo by Sam Baltrusis.*

A few months after the incident, I joined a group of tour guides who specialize in telling Boston's paranormal history, and it was there that I learned about many of the so-called ghosts from New England's past. While giving tours, including Boston Haunts, I had several encounters with the paranormal at the Omni Parker House.

During my first visit, for example, I heard a disembodied voice whisper "welcome" in my ear. Was it the hotel's founder, Harvey Parker?

Over the years, I've stayed away from the hotel because, from the outside, it had an inexplicably eerie vibe. While taking a photo in front of the famed "enchanted mirror" on the second-floor mezzanine, I noticed condensation mysteriously appear on the mirror as if someone, or something, was breathing on it. According to hotel lore, the antique was taken from Charles Dickens' room. He apparently stood in front of it to practice his nineteenth-century orations.

As a special treat for guests on my Boston Haunts ghost tour, I would guide them to the supernatural hot spot. While the ghost story is intriguing, what interested me even more is the fact that the press room next to the creepy mirror is where John F. Kennedy announced his candidacy for president. I've seen tons of photos and heard many stories from patrons who had strange encounters while staying on the hotel's upper floors. Today, the Omni Parker House has become one of my favorite haunts in the city. Haunted history oozes from the oldest continuously operating hotel in the country.

Besides being one of the more ornate structures in Boston, the Omni Parker House is also allegedly one of its most haunted. Originally built in October 1855, it boasts a slew of ghostly reports ranging from Harvey Parker himself—who passed away on May 31, 1884, at the age of seventy-nine and apparently continues to roam the halls of the hotel he built—to mysterious orbs floating down the tenth-floor corridor and a malevolent male spirit with a disturbing laugh who reportedly lingers in the recently reopened room 303.

Parker's rags-to-riches story started in 1826 when he moved to Boston with nothing but a pocketful of change. He saved his nickels and dimes while working as a coachman for a Brahmin socialite and built a restaurant that later became his namesake hotel. Torn down, except for one wing, and rebuilt in its present gilded glory in the late 1920s, the hotel was called the Parker House until the 1990s when the Omni hotel chain purchased the historic structure. The hotel has several claims to fame, including being the birthplace of the Boston cream pie. It also had a few famous employees, including Ho Chi Minh, who was a busboy, and Malcolm X, who worked as a waiter. John Wilkes Booth stayed at the Parker House eight days before assassinating President Lincoln on April 14, 1865. In fact, he used a shooting gallery not far from the hotel to practice his aim before heading to Ford's Theatre in Washington, D.C.

Other haunted happenings involve elevators mysteriously being called to the third floor—once frequented by both Charles Dickens and Henry Wadsworth Longfellow. The hotel's ornate lifts are known to mysteriously stop on the floor without anyone pushing a button. There's also the story of room 303, which in 1949 was the scene of a rumored suicide of a liquor salesman who killed himself with barbiturates and whiskey. According to lore, the room is said to have inspired horror legend Stephen King when he wrote the short-story-turned-film *1408*.

The Omni Parker House is a stone's throw to the extremely haunted Boston Common.

From its beginnings as a sheep and cow pasture in 1634, just a few years after the city itself was founded, the forty-eight-acre green space purchased from Boston's first settler, William Blackstone, has since been touted as the oldest city park in the United States. It's also home to some of the darker chapters from Boston's not-so-Puritanical past.

The Boston Common is chock-full of ghosts, graves and gallows. It is, in essence, "one big anonymous burying ground," wrote Holly Nadler, author of *Ghosts of Boston Town*. "Under the Puritan regime, untold numbers of miscreants—murderers, thieves, pirates, Indians, deserters, Quakers and putative witches—were executed in the Common" at the so-called Great Elm, which was also nicknamed by locals as the hanging or gallows tree. "At risk to their own lives, friends and family might sneak in under the cover of darkness, cut down the cadaver and bury it somewhere in the park," continued Nadler. "If no one came forward to deal with the disastrous remains, town officials disposed of them in the river, where bloated bodies frequently washed in and out with the tides."

There was also a mass grave site near the southern corner of the Common, yards away from the designated Central Burying Ground. In early 1895, the human remains of one hundred dead bodies were uncovered during the excavation of the nation's first underground trolley station, now the Boylston Green Line stop. A mob scene of "curiosity seekers" lined up along the Boylston Street corner of the Common "looking at the upturning of the soil," according to the April 18, 1895, edition of the *Boston Daily Globe*. The report continued, saying that "a large number of human bones and skulls are being unearthed as the digging on the Boylston Street mall" progressed. Thrill-seeking spectators were horrified by the sights and smells emanating from the site and were forced to move by early May.

Several haunted cemeteries dot the Boston Common, including King's Chapel Burying Ground and the paranormally active Central Burying Ground. *Photo by Frank C. Grace.*

And that was just the first round of skeletons in the Common's collective closet. As the excavation continued, officials uncovered the remains of hundreds—some historians estimated between 900 and 1,100 bodies—buried in shallow graves beneath the Boylston mall.

While the nearby Granary Burial Ground earns top billing thanks to its Freedom Trail–friendly names, including Paul Revere, Samuel Adams, John Hancock and even Mother Goose, the Boston Common's lesser-known Central Burying Ground has something that the other graveyards don't: ghosts. After Boston's Puritan leaders purchased the plot in 1756, the cemetery was used as a final resting spot for foreigners and other paupers who couldn't cough up enough shillings for a proper burial. The graveyard is the resting spot for composer William Billings and artist Gilbert Stuart, who was responsible for painting George Washington's mug on the dollar bill. It is also reportedly the place where the see-through denizens from the Common's spirit realm prefer to hang out.

"Visitors to the graveyard have reported seeing shadowy figures appear nearby, often near trees," wrote Christopher Forest in *Boston's Haunted History*. "The figures disappear or dissolve when people look right at them. Some people have associated the figures with the former hanging victims who met their end on the Boston Common gallows."

Apparently, the cemetery's spirits like to have fun with tourists. "They have been accused of poking people in the back, rattling keys and even brushing up against shoulders. Some people roaming the graveyard have reported being grabbed from behind by an unseen force," he wrote.

Jeffrey Doucette, a veteran tour guide, said he was a skeptic until he witnessed a woman have a close encounter with a paranormal force outside the cemetery's gates in 2011. "She felt someone or something tap her on the shoulder," he mused. "She looked annoyed, and I had to assure her that no one was there."

The more notorious haunting at the Central Burying Ground centers on a young female spirit who was described by the late ghost expert Jim McCabe as a teen girl "with long red hair, sunken cheekbones and a mud-splattered gray dress on." On a rainy afternoon in the 1970s, she paid a visit to a dentist named Dr. Matt Rutger, who reportedly experienced "a total deviation from reality as most of us know it." According to Nadler's *Ghosts of Boston Town*, Rutger was checking out the gravestone carvings. He felt a tap on his shoulder and then a violent yank on his collar. No one was there.

As Rutger was bolting from the cemetery, he noticed something out of the corner of his eye. "I saw a young girl standing motionless in the rear corner of the cemetery, staring at me intently," he said. The mischievous spirit then reappeared near the graveyard's gate, almost fifty yards from the initial encounter. Then the unthinkable happened. "He somehow made it by her to Boylston Street, and even though he couldn't see her, he felt her hand slip inside his coat pocket, take out his keys and dangle them in midair before dropping them," McCabe recounted.

Rutger, in an interview with Nadler, said the '70s-era paranormal encounter has left an indelible mark on his psyche. "One thing is certain, the encounter affected me in very profound ways," he reflected. "As a trained medical professional, I have always seen the world in fairly empirical terms. There's no way something like that cannot completely change how you think about the world."

Based on the freaked-out expression on Haunted Boston tour guide Jeffrey Doucette's face, he looked as if he had just seen a ghost. "You're not going to believe what just happened," he said, rushing into the Omni Parker House's mezzanine watering hole, Parker's Bar, one Sunday evening after giving a ghost tour to a group of high school kids from Vermont. "As I was telling a story at the site of the hanging elm, I could tell something was up," he recalled, packing up his lantern and sitting down at a cozy table near the bar's fireplace. "The chaperone is waving at me as if 'Jeff, you need to look at this,' and she shows me her camera. I literally couldn't believe what I was seeing. In the photo, it looks like seven nooses hanging from the trees in the area near what was the hanging tree."

Doucette, a popular tour guide among out-of-town visitors thanks to his distinct Boston accent, said he was a skeptic for years until he had a few close encounters of the paranormal kind while trudging through the tour's haunted sites scattered throughout the Boston Common and Beacon Hill. Now, he's a full-fledged believer. "I was like, 'What the...? Let's get out of here,'" he said, referring to the noose photo taken earlier in the evening and creepy pictures of demonic, red-colored orbs shot in the Central Burying Ground. "It literally freaked me out. This year, I've seen a lot of orbs, but nothing like what I just saw. I'm not sure if [the spirits] heard me talking about the interview I'm having with you, but they really showed their colors tonight. The ghosts in the Boston Common were out in full force, and they were screaming."

The tour guide, who works in the finance department at a publishing house in Government Center when he's not moonlighting with Haunted Boston, said he was raised in a superstitious Irish Catholic family. "My grandmother was a tinker, or an Irish gypsy, and she would go to confession and then she would read Tarot cards to make sure she was covering both ends of the spectrum," he joked. "I suspect a little of that tinker mysticism was passed on to me. My mother would always say people would die in threes. When someone passed, we made sure we left the windows open to let the spirits out."

Doucette was an amused skeptic until he gave his first Boston Common tour in 2009. "A kid on the tour shot a photo of me, and there were all of these white orbs near the Great Elm site," he explained. "The last photo really threw me for a loop. It was of me with a green light coming out of my belly, and I was freaked out. Since then, we've had a few orbs here and there, but this year has been out of control. Tonight, I really don't know what happened. Will I sleep? I don't know. But it was something that I've never experienced before."

The tour guide said he reached out to a psychic who told him that the green light emanating from his torso was an indication that the spirits in the Boston Common liked the way he told their stories. "At the hanging elm, many of the people who were hanged there were done so unjustifiably by the Puritans for crimes they didn't commit. If anyone disagreed with the status quo at that time, they were executed. Boston was founded by Puritans, and it was either their way or the highway ... or the hangman's noose. Even in the modern age, if you disagree with authority, there's the chance that you can be shamed. In my opinion, many of those hanged in the Boston Common were victims of freedom of speech and died at the hands of oppressive authority figures. So when I say on the tour that many of the people hanged at the Great Elm site died innocently, I feel like I'm giving them a voice."

Doucette continued, "I've always been respectful of the spirits in the Boston Common. They've never bothered me at home, and I never had an issue with a haunting. But when I do the tours, they do come out. I've been a strong advocate for those who were disenfranchised and oppressed, especially women, and they always respond to the stories that I tell on the tour."

As far as historical figures are concerned, Doucette said he's drawn to people like Ann "Goody" Glover, who was hanged for allegedly practicing witchcraft on November 16, 1688. Glover, a self-sufficient, strong-willed Irishwoman who spoke fluent Gaelic, lived in the North End, where she washed laundry for John Goodwin and his family. After a spirited spat in her native Gaelic tongue with Goodwin's 13-year-old daughter, Martha, Glover was accused of bewitching the four children in the household and was sent to prison for practicing the dark arts. While Glover was exonerated of her crimes in 1988 and dubbed a "Catholic martyr" three hundred years after her execution, Doucette said he's compelled to tell her story. However, he's not convinced that Glover's spirit is haunting the Boston Common. "People want a big name to associate with the hauntings in the Common, but I seriously don't think that's the case," adding that "it makes for good storytelling."

Doucette, who ends the Haunted Boston ghost tour at the historic Omni Parker House located at 60 School St. near Park Street station, said he's heard many creepy tales while hanging out at Parker's Bar. "I spend a huge amount of time here," he remarked. "There was a night in October, and I came into the bar before a tour. A woman who was in her mid-fifties and working the bar asked if I gave the haunted tour and then told me the creepiest story." According to the Parker's Bar worker, one guest checked in but had a hard time checking out. There was an early-season snowstorm, and the Parker House guest refused to pay his hotel bill. "As he was leaving and coming out of the School Street entrance, the doormat mysteriously flies up and blocks the exit as he's trying to leave," the tour guide mused. "The guy turns around and pays his bill."

Like Doucette, the man who tried to leave the Parker House without paying his bill was smacked in the face with what could have been a ghost from Boston's past. "Our history has many skeletons in its closet, and the spirits want their story to be told," he said. "I'm giving a voice to those without a voice."

CONCLUSION

"Some have seen her, and others have just seen the chair cushions in that section move. Those that have seen the ghost say that she resembles a woman from the 1920s or a flapper."

—IAN JUDGE, SOMERVILLE THEATRE

If I had to pick to pick two cities that should be on the *13 Most Haunted in Massachusetts'* honorable mention list it would be Somerville and Malden. Of course, I'm biased. I've lived in Somerville for years and I'm the coordinator of a citizen journalism project for Malden Access TV.

When it comes to the most haunted in the state, there's no place like home.

I had my first spirited encounter as an adult while living in Somerville's Ball Square in the early 1990s. I recall seeing an apparition of a young girl who would play hide-and-seek in the hallway. She was a mischievous poltergeist, and I remember hearing phantom footsteps leading to our second-floor apartment.

Since returning to Somerville in 2007, I've spent years investigating alleged accounts of paranormal activity at sites all over New England. I've collected a slew of reports from these supposedly haunted locales, and the mission was to give readers a contemporary take on the bevy of site-specific legends. My *13 Most Haunted in Massachusetts* book is, in essence, a supernatural-themed travel guide written with a historical lens.

While researching my third book *Ghosts of Salem: Haunts of the Witch City* in 2013, I managed a pop-up Spirit Halloween store in what would become my new neighborhood in Somerville's Assembly Square. The seasonal shop was located in an abandoned Circuit City building and had a history of squatters and vandals before it became a Halloween store. During my initial interview, a manager from another region asked me about my books. I told her.

She looked at me and sheepishly said: "You know this place is haunted, right?" I laughed. Why would a former Circuit City have paranormal activity? She told me that several employees had heard inexplicable phantom footsteps in the back storage area near the loading dock. She said that some of the store's animatronics would mysteriously turn on and off. Shadow figures were seen through the glass. She also heard what sounded like residual gunshots in the storage area.

The idea of a haunted Halloween store seemed a bit too good to be true. However, she was right. I regularly heard mysterious footsteps in the back area. I also experienced recurring poltergeist activity that involved one of our props, a creepy plastic rat.

The ghosts of Spirit Halloween were trying to tell me something and it involved a rat or, in '50s-era speak, a snitch. Before closing the store, I would check to see if all of our decor was shelved appropriately. I especially kept an eye on our creepy-crawler section, which included stuffed rats and a larger-than-life plastic rodent.

I also had to set the alarm so there was no way anybody could have been playing a practical joke. The following morning, without fail, I would open and find a rat strategically placed somewhere in the store. It became a daily ritual of sorts that I jokingly called "find the rat."

In 2015, I returned to Somerville's haunted Halloween store and the residual energy still lingered there. Why return? I recently moved into the new Assembly Row apartment complex facing the Mystic River and I decided to make a comeback as Spirit Halloween's store manager. It's easy access.

Spot the rat? A pop-up Spirit Halloween store in Somerville's Assembly Square is allegedly haunted by a disgruntled spirit. *Photo by Sam Baltrusis.*

I talked with people who worked in the building when it was a Circuit City and one woman claimed that she regularly heard phantom footsteps. "Yeah, I always thought this place was haunted," she said. "I'm not surprised it's a Halloween store. I bet the ghosts are having fun here."

One Spirit Halloween employee, Christine Broderick, claimed she had a close encounter with the ghost in the loading dock area. "I was in the warehouse breaking up boxes and my hair got pulled hard and I saw a man standing a few feet away. He was probably about 5'11" and had light brown, blondish hair," Broderick recalled. "I screamed. He disappeared. I'm starting to get freaked out because I don't know why he doesn't like me?"

Assembly Square got its name from the Ford Motor Company's assembly plant built there in 1926. It was also a hub for the Boston and Maine Railroad. The assembly plant closed in 1958, and the initial theory was that the ghosts were somehow tied to the plant.

Somerville also has a history of modern-era gangsters, so "the rat" may literally be mob related. Of course, the notorious James "Whitey" Bulger is making headlines again thanks to Johnny Depp's performance in the movie *Black Mass*. Bulger earned his Winter Hill Gang moniker from the Winter Hill neighborhood, which is right next to Assembly Square. Truthfully, Bulger did most of his seedy, underworld activity in South Boston but he definitely spent time in what is now my new neighborhood in Somerville.

I've been told by multiple people that a hush-hush crime happened in the building. According to local lore, a criminal hid in the building and was found by police. "My dad said that a guy escaped from prison and was found in the loading dock area," said one of my employees, Brittany Dean. "Cops found him there and shot him."

While the story is unsubstantiated, it would explain some of the activity in the loading dock area, including the phantom steps and inexplicable gunshot sounds. It's as if the murder of the man is a residual haunting or a videotaped replay of tragic, past events.

However, things also have been mysteriously moved throughout the location. Based on my experience, I would categorize the haunting as a "stay behind," a type of spirit that doesn't know he's dead due to the circumstances of his death.

The late Dr. Hans Holzer, in an interview in 2005, explained the phenomenon. "'Stay behinds' are relatively common," he said. "Somebody dies, and then they're really surprised that all of a sudden they're not dead. They're alive like they were. They don't understand it because they weren't prepared for it. So they go back to what they knew most—their chair, their room, and they just sit there. Next, they want to let people know that they're still 'alive.' So they'll do little things like moving things, appear to relatives, pushing objects, poltergeist phenomena, and so on."

I've had several encounters with "stay behinds" in Somerville. The first was a female spirit I jokingly called "scissor sister."

Before moving into Assembly Row, I fled my room with a "boo!" in Somerville's Davis Square. The house's resident ghost, a playful older female poltergeist with an affinity for scissors, did various things in the house to make her presence known. According to a psychic who visited the two-floor Gothic-decorated haunt, she was a seamstress during the Depression era. While I was writing my first book, *Ghosts of Boston*, an unseen force opened doors that were firmly shut and lights mysteriously turned on and off without provocation. One night, I spotted a full-bodied apparition of a gray-haired female figure wearing an old-school white nightgown and donning fuzzy slippers dart across the first floor while I stood, in shock, at the top of the stairs.

The ghostly incidents escalated after the initial encounter. While I was preparing for the launch party for my first book at Boston's Old South Meeting House, the scissors sitting on the front-room table mysteriously started to spin, and one night, during an interview with Paranormal State's Ryan Buell's *Paranormal Insider Radio*, I heard a loud knock on my bedroom door. I quickly opened it, but no one was there. Oddly, the phantom knocking continued throughout the phone interview. I wasn't afraid.

The gig was up. I decided to move.

Master psychic Denise Fix picked up on the spirit of the seamstress during our second interview. "She's not trying to scare you. She wants your attention," Fix said, sitting at a table that, oddly, was a repurposed Singer sewing machine. "She sewed for many people and felt quite tortured a lot of the time. She was celebrated by you, and she thanks you for that. She was released from whatever bound her there," Fix continued. "And it wasn't a good thing to be bound there."

Two weeks later, I moved out. My last night in the house was memorable. My roommate's exotic parrot escaped from its cage and perched on the oven's open flame. The bird was quickly engulfed in flames but didn't catch fire. While carrying boxes down the stairs, I slipped. I felt something hold me back as I watched the box fall down the stairs. Glass shattered. It could have been me. I fled the haunted house on Hall Avenue and haven't looked back.

I'm often asked what is the most haunted hot spot in my home city? I say without hesitation that it's the Somerville Theatre in Davis Square.

If the ominous red-eyed owls peering from the historic theater's marquee and peeking out from the labyrinthine hallways aren't enough to give you the chills, then its ghost lore involving a 1920s-era flapper will have your hair standing on end.

Built in 1914 by the Boston-based firm Funk & Wilcox, the Somerville Theatre was originally designed for stage shows, opera, vaudeville and, eventually, motion pictures. Before the Depression, the building boasted a basement café, bowling alley, billiards hall and the Hobbs Crystal Ballroom, a large dance space on the second floor that could easily host up to 700 foxtrotting partygoers. During its vaudeville heyday in 1915, the stage had its own stock company, the Somerville Theatre Players, and welcomed future icons like Tallulah Bankhead, Francis X. Bushman and Ray Bolger, who played the Scarecrow in MGM's *The Wizard of Oz*. Kay Corbett, who was part of the vaudeville-era sister act known as the Corbett Revue, also regularly appeared.

Apparently, the schedule was grueling for the Somerville Players. They launched a new play each week and performed twice a day. "We rehearse every morning from nine till twelve and then lunch, then a matinee every day, then dinner, then evening performances," wrote Bankhead in a letter to her grandfather dated 1919. "I'm nearly dead now and I have only been here a week."

A ghostly flapper is said to inhabit rows J and K in the main theater's orchestra-right section of the Somerville Theatre in Davis Square. *Photo by Frank C. Grace.*

For its grand opening on May 11, 1914, the one-thousand-plus-seat auditorium showcased a bevy of live acts, including the Stewart Sisters, a comedy skit from the Fuller-Rose company called A King for a Day, singing by the Adairs and a two-reel film presentation of The Inventor's Wife. Joseph Hobbs, who leased and eventually sold the theater to Arthur F. Viano in 1926, hired an up-and-comer and future film director Busby Berkeley, who went on to produce a slew of stylish musicals including *42nd Street.* The entertainment complex was a featured stop for seventeen years until the Depression's economic tumult forced it to become a movies-only establishment in 1932.

It's around this time that a ghost from its vaudeville past returned to claim her favorite seat in the main auditorium. "The story which has been told to me by two different unrelated sources is that there's an apparition around rows J and K in the orchestra-right section of the main theater here, which was built for movies and vaudeville in 1914," said Ian Judge, the director of operations at the Somerville Theatre. "Some have seen her, and others have just seen the chair cushions in that section move. Those that have seen the ghost say that she resembles a woman from the 1920s or a flapper."

Judge, who eventually got validation about the haunting from a former office manager and a previous lessee, Galen Daly, said he had a close encounter with the flapper ghost when he first started his job more than one decade ago. "While I have never seen an apparition, I did see the seats move in a hard-to-explain way," Judge explained. "I was doing some cleaning and renovation work overnight in the balcony. I was all alone, not another person in the building. As I was cleaning, I heard the sound of the seat cushions moving, as if someone were bouncing them up and down … they fold up, as theater seats often do. I rushed to the edge of the balcony and looked down and saw two of the seat cushions moving up and down, and they came to a stop as I watched. There was nobody else there, and nobody went out any of the exit doors."

The director of operations said he hadn't heard any stories about the flapper ghost until years after his close encounter. "I've never experienced anything since then, even though I've been alone here hundreds of times," Judge said. "I guess perhaps it was just the ghost welcoming me to my new job."

So, why haunted theaters? Holly Nadler, author of *Ghosts of Boston Town*, believes it's the romantic aesthetic. "All old and beautiful theaters look haunted, with their shadowy corridors, flickering lanterns, vaulted ceilings and Gothic ornaments," she wrote. "They also sound haunted, from the creaking of the woodwork, the rustling of old pipes, the sighs of air currents trapped inside thick stone walls. And indeed, there are some who contend that all old and beautiful theaters really are haunted."

Judge, among the believers, said he's still spooked. However, he has no clue who or what haunts the Somerville Theatre. "I don't know," he said when asked about the ghost's identity. "While nobody has ever died here that we know of, perhaps those were her favorite seats? Back in the days when we also had a stock theater company performing on stage around the movie season, people likely had reserved or favorite seats. Maybe she was a matinee-idol fan?"

One theory involves a former ticket seller, a die-hard fan of the Somerville Theatre and regular attendee of the stock theater company until she lost her vision. Sallie B. Irish, 28 years old, committed suicide by jumping out of a fourth-story window in the Back Bay on May 10, 1923. "She had a nervous breakdown, involving trouble with her eyes, since which time she had worked [at the Somerville Theatre] only occasionally," reported the *Boston Daily Globe*. Irish apparently loved the theater and became hysterical when she started having vision problems. She was found dead on Massachusetts Avenue after jumping from her bedroom window. "Miss Irish was very popular about the Somerville Theatre and with its patrons, having worked there eight years," the *Globe* continued.

Perhaps Irish has made a postmortem return to her favorite seats in the main theater? Yes, all the world's a stage … and all the lingering spirits merely players.

In addition to Somerville, Malden is a city with an inexplicably large number of wayward spirits and residual hauntings.

Sure, it's not a typically haunted city and deviates a bit from the Lizzie Borden or Salem witch city norm. However, there's a historical legacy that's often overlooked by ghost hunters and para-celebs. It's also an easy Orange Line train ride from Boston and my home in Somerville's Assembly Square.

During the winter, I was covering an event in the old wing of the historic Malden Public Library. The well-preserved throwback to the gilded age was recently featured in the movie *Ted 2*, with Mark Wahlberg, and served as a creepy backdrop for a Travel Channel's *Dead Files* episode called *Dark Inheritance*.

While taking photos for MATV's *Neighborhood View*, I swear I spotted a chair move in the Converse Memorial Building as if an invisible force was taking a seat at the old-school library built in 1885.

"On its walls hang several of the paintings that were there when the building was dedicated in 1885," explained the library's website. "Most prominent is a full-length portrait of 17-year-old Frank Converse, in whose memory the library was constructed. On either side of him are his parents and the building's donors, Elisha and Mary Converse."

Was the spirit I encountered the ghost of the 17-year-old Converse teen? Digging through some historical research, it turns out that Frank Converse died tragically in what is believed to be the first bank robbery in America. The town's postmaster, Edward Green, was desperate for money and on Dec. 15, 1865, he trekked through the snowy streets of Malden to the city's bank located at 48 Pleasant St. Green was there to make a usual deposit but noticed the teen was alone. The soon-to-be bank robber returned from the post office with his recently purchased Smith and Wesson pistol.

America's first bank robber shot Converse in the left temple. The boy fell to the ground and Green, who stole $5,000 from the Malden Bank, shot Converse again.

The murder made national headlines. Green confessed to the grisly crime two months after the boy's body was discovered. Green was sentenced to death and was hanged in April 1866. Converse's wealthy father, Elisha, became the first mayor of Malden in 1882 and erected the library three years later in honor of his slain son.

For the record, the murder occurred a stone's throw away from the library, which is located at 36 Salem St. Others who visit the historic landmark claim to have encountered unseen forces move furniture and even reach out to creeped-out patrons. "The library has a basement that contains books in different languages. I once went [there] and was looking for a certain book. All I could feel is a hand on the back of my neck," reported Vian on the *Ghosts of America* website. "It bothered me so much. As soon as I moved a little it stopped. Then after at least 10 seconds the hand went back on my neck and it was the most terrifying thing I've ever experienced."

Yes, Malden boasts a bone-chilling assortment of ghostly hot spots rumored to be stomping grounds for spirits ... and not one of those El Diablo concoctions at Ferry Street Food & Drink.

The Malden Public Library was recently featured in the movie
Ted 2 and served as a creepy backdrop for a Travel Channel's *Dead
Files* episode called *Dark Inheritance*. *Photo by Sam Baltrusis.*

Speaking of the new restaurant formerly occupied by watering holes like Jimmy O'Keefe's, the Shamrock Inn and No 9 Ale House, Ferry Street Food & Drink located at 118 Ferry St. made headlines in 2013 about a resident ghost rumored to still claim his bar stool in the afterlife.

According to lore, the left-behind ghost looked like John Candy's "Uncle Buck" character. The spirit supposedly slipped and died in the basement when the space was Jimmy O'Keefe's.

Shannon Ladd, Ferry Street's co-owner, claimed that she recently had a close encounter with the Uncle Buck ghost. "Your timing is impeccable because (not) until last night did we have that hair-stand-up feeling, but nothing has happened," said Ladd. "Then last night around midnight, for the first time I saw something move on the opposite side of the basement and I swore someone was there. But everyone had left except myself and Jason (Ladd's husband) and Jason was upstairs."

Ladd continued: "We took over the space in March, so maybe he was just shy until now. To be honest, I pretty much just ran up the stairs and got out of there! He hasn't shown up on his bar stool just yet, but we do have bar stools stored in the basement."

Sharon Santillo, a resident of the former Belmont School on Cross Street, says her fellow tenants encountered a ghost girl when they moved in 10 years ago.

"My condo building was converted from a school that had been built in the late 1800s and added onto in 1930s," Santillo recalled. "All the tenants moved in around the same time and two people on the ground floor saw a ghost of a young girl. She had long dark hair and did not seem upset nor were they frightened by her."

Santillo said the girl was spotted near the school's former theater. "Someone who had been a teacher in the building told us the area where she was seen had been the stage end of the cafeteria back when the building was a school," she said. "We made up a story about her that she had happily acted in school plays and came back to be in that place of good memories. But the conversion of the building took away that stage and the girl has not been back since those early months, that I have heard about anyway."

Michael Baker, a well-respected paranormal investigator with Para-Boston and featured expert in my first book *Ghosts of Boston*, said Malden has several ghost stories including the "Lady in Grey" specter at Holy Cross Cemetery. "There is a ghostly hitchhiker that has been picked up several times only to disappear once she is inside the car," Baker said. "I know that is a popular theme for cemetery haunts, but this one comes from the '60s."

Bell Rock Cemetery is home to the "walking corpse of Malden" and Holy Cross Cemetery boasts the "Lady in Grey," a ghostly hitchhiker that disappears after she's picked up. *Photo by Frank C. Grace.*

There's also the legend of the mad scientist buried in Bell Rock Cemetery, which has a gravestone dating back to 1670, known as the Walking Corpse of Malden. The scientist experimented with chemicals to keep his post-mortem flesh from rotting. "A group of people opened up the mad scientist's tomb after several years and were shocked and amazed to find that his flesh had not decayed as expected," according to the the legend. "A medical student impetuously decided to sneak into the tomb that night and try to steal the corpse's head, but was tormented by apparitions and frantically ran out of the cemetery. He tossed the severed head into the tomb, and it is believed that a headless ghost walked the cemetery at night searching for its missing head."

Baker says he heard several creepy stories about the now-closed Malden Hospital being haunted. "A nurse friend of mine who passed away a few years ago used to tell me about crying that she would hear coming from a room that was vacant on the third floor," he said. "She told me that several other nurses noticed the nurse call light coming on from that room during the night shifts when the room was empty. She claims that she wasn't the only one to hear the crying and described it as a cry of pain ... sort of a moaning. "

Baker continued: "She also said that the freight elevator would sometimes take you to the third floor no matter which floor number you hit."

The paranormal expert also overheard a ghost story at a store in the space formerly occupied by the Granada Theatre located near the corner of Pleasant and Main streets in Malden Square.

"I overheard a couple of the employees talking about a sighting of a man with a cape and a strange hat," Baker recalls. "They were arguing about where they thought he was from. I then found out that what they were talking about was a ghostly apparition that one of the employees saw when they came in to open in the morning. The employee had to go home because she was so shaken up."

The former pharmacy was in the exact 21 Pleasant St. spot that housed the former Granada. For the record, the allegedly haunted theater closed in the mid-'80s and was later demolished after two girls snuck in the building in 1987 and set a fire that destroyed the historic structure.

Yes, the show must go on ... even in the afterlife.

SOURCES

Updated excerpts from my first three books including *Ghosts of Boston: Haunts of the Hub* and *Ghosts of Salem: Haunts of the Witch City* were featured in *13 Most Haunted in Massachusetts*. The material in this book is drawn from published sources, including issues of *Boston Spirit*, *Stuff* magazine, *Boston Globe*, *Boston Herald*, *Metrowest Daily*, *The New York Times*, *Patriot Ledger*, *SouthCoast Today*, MATV's *Neighborhood View* and television programs like the Travel Channel's *Ghost Adventures* and Syfy's *Ghost Hunters*. Several books on the Bay State's paranormal history were used and cited throughout the text. Other New England–based websites and periodicals, like my various newspaper and magazine articles on the paranormal, Joni Mayhan's work for *Ghost Diaries* and Peter Muise's blog *New England Folklore* served as primary sources. I also conducted firsthand interviews, and some of the material is drawn from my own research. The Boston-based ghost tour, Boston Haunts, was also a major source and generated original content. My tours in Salem, Cambridge, Boston Harbor and Provincetown also served as inspiration for the book. It should be noted that ghost stories are subjective, and I have made a concerted effort to stick to the historical facts, even if it resulted in debunking an alleged encounter with the paranormal.

Baltrusis, Sam. *Ghosts of Boston: Haunts of the Hub*. Charleston, SC: The History Press, 2012.

Baltrusis, Sam. *Ghosts of Cambridge: Haunts of Harvard Square and Beyond*. Charleston, SC: The History Press, 2013.

Baltrusis, Sam. *Ghosts of Salem: Haunts of the Witch City*. Charleston, SC: The History Press, 2014.

Balzano, Christopher. *Dark Woods: Cults, Crime, and the Paranormal in the Freetown State Forest, Massachusetts*. Atglen, PA: Schiffer Publishing, 2007.

D'Agostino, Thomas. *A Guide to Haunted New England*. Charleston, SC: The History Press, 2009.

Forest, Christopher. *North Shore Spirits of Massachusetts*. Atglen, PA: Schiffer Publishing, 2003.

Gellerman, Bruce and Sherman, Erik. *Massachusetts Curiosities*. Guilford, CT: The Globe Pequot Press, 2005.

Hall, Thomas. *Shipwrecks of Massachusetts Bay*. Charleston, SC: The History Press, 2012.

Hauk, Dennis William. *Haunted Places: The National Directory*. New York: Penguin Group, 1996.

Jasper, Mark. *Haunted Cape Cod & The Islands*. Yarmouthport, MA: On Cape Publications, 2002.

Jasper, Mark. *Haunted Inns of New England*. Yarmouthport, MA: On Cape Publications, 2000.

Mayhan, Joni. *Bones in the Basement*. Gardner, MA: Joni Mayhan, 2014.

Muise, Peter. *Legends and Lore of the North Shore*. Charleston, SC: The History Press, 2014.

Nadler, Holly Mascott. *Ghosts of Boston Town: Three Centuries of True Hauntings.* Camden, ME: Down East Books, 2002.

Norman, Michael and Scott, Beth. *Historic Haunted America.* New York, NY: Tor Books, 1995.

Ogden, Tom. *The Complete Idiot's Guide to Ghosts & Hauntings.* Indianapolis, IN: Alpha Books, 2004.

Revai, Cheri. *Haunted Massachusetts: Ghosts and Strange Phenomena of the Bay State.* Mechanicsburg, PA: Stackpole Books, 2005.

Summers, Ken. *Queer Hauntings: True Tales of Gay & Lesbian Ghosts.* Mapleshade, NJ: Lethe Press, 2009.

ABOUT THE AUTHOR

$\mathbf{S}$am Baltrusis, author of *Ghosts of Boston: Haunts of the Hub* and *Ghosts of Salem: Haunts of the Witch City*, is the former editor-in-chief of *Spare Change News* and teaches journalism classes at Malden Access TV (MATV). He has been featured as Boston's paranormal expert on the Biography Channel's *Haunted Encounters* and *Paranormal State's* Ryan Buell's *Paranormal Insider Radio*. As a side gig, Baltrusis moonlights as a guide and launched the successful ghost tours, Boston Haunts and Cambridge Haunts. In October 2014, he spearheaded a boat tour called *Haunted Boston Harbor*. Baltrusis is also a sought-after lecturer who speaks at dozens of paranormal-related events scattered throughout New England. In the past, he's worked for VH1, MTV.com, *Newsweek*, ABC Radio and as a regional stringer for *The New York Times*.

After a road trip to some of the state's most haunted locations,
author Sam Baltrusis enjoys a breathtaking view from the Wigwam
Western Summit in North Adams. *Photo by Frank C. Grace.*

Made in the USA
Las Vegas, NV
16 December 2021

38268594R00075